Sharing Visions

Divine Revelations, Angels,
And Holy Coincidences

Cycle C

John E. Sumwalt, Editor

with

*Ralph Milton, Kerri Sherwood, Cheryl Kirking,
Lee Domann, Rosmarie Trapp, Jo Perry-Sumwalt,
Pamela J. Tinnen, Linda J. Vogel, and others*

CSS Publishing Company, Inc., Lima, Ohio

SHARING VISIONS

Scripture quotations marked (NRSV) are from the *New Revised Standard Version of the
Bible*, copyright 1989 by the Division of Christian Education of the National Council of
the Churches of Christ in the USA. Used by permission.

Library of Congress Cataloging-in-Publication Data

Sumwalt, John E.
    Sharing visions : divine revelations, angels, and holy coincidences, Cycle C / John E.
Sumwalt, editor ; with Ralph Milton ... [et al.].
        p. cm.
    ISBN 0-7880-1970-8 (pbk. : alk. paper)
    1. Miracles 2. Visions. 3. Common lectionary (1992). Year C. I. Sumwalt, John E. II.
Milton, Ralph. III. Title.
    BT97.3.S86   2003
248.2'9—dc21
                                                                              2003004771

For more information about CSS Publishing Company resources, visit our website at
www.csspub.com or e-mail us at custserv@csspub.com or call (800) 241-4056.

ISBN 0-7880-1970-8   PRINTED IN U.S.A.

In loving memory
of my dear aunt,
Kathryne Long Ballard

Table Of Contents

Holy Week And Easter

Pentecost

Acknowledgments

It has been a joy to work with the 84 contributors to this second volume of vision stories. It is an honor and a privilege to have a part in the sharing of these witnesses. My thanks to each one of them for entrusting me with their sacred stories.

I am thankful for the encouragement and support of our publisher, Wesley Runk; our editors, Teresa Rhoads and Stan Purdum; and to Ellen Shockey, Tim Runk, Jonathon Smith, David Jordan-Squire, Dee Norton, and the rest of the hardworking CSS team.

The book would not have been possible without the wisdom and hard work of my writing partner of 28 years, Jo Perry-Sumwalt. She is a kind and loving editor, more than I deserve. I am continually blessed by her love and that of our children, Kati and Orrin.

Special thanks to our colleagues on the Wauwatosa Avenue Church staff, Carol Smith, Mary Peterson, Janice Beutin, and Jodie Hunt.

When Visions Are Rare

Now the boy Samuel was ministering to the Lord
under Eli. The word of the Lord was rare in those
days; visions were not widespread.

These words mark the beginning of one of the most dramatic visions recorded in scripture. Was the word of the Lord rare in those days or was there no one who was able to hear and see? Elizabeth Barrett Browning wrote:

Earth's crammed with heaven,
And every common bush afire with God;
But only he who seeks takes off his shoes;
The rest sit round and pluck blackberries.[1]

There is much plucking of blackberries in our world today. And those who do see the fire, and dare to speak of it, are usually discouraged by well-meaning church leaders.

In the opening scene of the 1999 film, *The Messenger: The Story of Joan of Arc*, a very young Jeanne d'Arc is shown entering the confessional of a small country chapel. The priest is a little annoyed because she has already been to confession that day. He says to her, "Why are you so often in church?"

"I feel safe here ... I try to talk to him. Mostly he's the one who does the talking."

"... What does he say to you?"

"He says I must be good and help everyone ... Do you think he is coming in the sky?"

The priest, like Samuel's mentor, Eli, finally figures out who is talking to Joan and then he speaks to her in a soft, gentle voice saying, "Perhaps, but wherever he is coming from, I think you should listen to him. I think he is giving you very good advice."[2]

I show this excerpt in the seminars I lead on telling visions after I have read the story of Samuel's call in the temple. And I ask, "How do you suppose Joan would be treated if she shared her visions in the office of your pastor or in a Sunday school classroom in your church? Would she be encouraged to listen and to be open to the voice of God? Would you or other leaders in your church encourage a young person like Samuel to invite God to speak after hearing God call his name?"

Marcus Borg writes in his book, *The God We Never Knew*: "In a number of workshops, I have asked people whether they have had one or more experiences that they would identify as an experience of God and, if so, to share them in small groups. On average 80 percent of the participants identify one or more and are eager to talk about them. They also frequently report that they had never been asked that question in a church setting or given an opportunity to talk about it."[3]

Dorothee Soelle, who once taught at a theological seminary in New York, tells how the students responded when asked to talk about their religious experience. "There was an embarrassed silence; it was as if we had asked our grandmothers to talk about their sex life." Then, she says, one brave young woman spoke of a wonderful moment of happiness she had one night while looking at the stars, "... a feeling of overwhelming clarity, of being sheltered and carried." Soelle adds, "Suppose that young woman had lived in fourteenth-century Flanders; she would have had at her disposal other traditions of language allowing her to say, 'I heard a voice,' or 'I saw a light ...' Our culture confines her to sobriety, self-restriction, and scholarly manners of expression. How she fought these constraints and the very fact that she did makes her unforgettable."[4]

How could this happen in a church whose life is guided by scriptures filled with vision stories like Samuel's? It is not that visions are any more rare in our own time than in Samuel's; it's that most of us have not felt safe enough to talk about our experiences of God's presence, in church or anywhere else. How could this happen in a church founded on mystical propositions like "resurrection," "Holy Spirit," the presence of Christ in the Eucharist,

14

and the promise of Jesus that "where two or three are gathered in my name, I am there among them" (Matthew 18:20)?

William Johnston wrote: "Assuredly, Western Christianity has a rich mystical tradition. But how often were mystics ignored or marginalized or persecuted by an establishment that put emphasis on words and letters, on doctrines and dogmas, on the strict observance of church law? ... The tragedy of Western Christianity is that there were, and are, so few mystics in the establishment."[5]

Even when church leaders have visions they are reluctant to share them. "At the height of his illness in 1954, Pope Pius XII had a vision of Christ in which the Savior spoke to him in 'his own true voice.' The Vatican kept Pope Pius' revelation secret for nearly a year, then through the 'affectionate indiscretion' of one of the Holy Father's close friends, the picture magazine *Oggi* broke the story in its November 19, 1955 issue."[6]

The nonreligious are just as reluctant to report their experiences of the holy. A. J. Ayers, the British philosopher who introduced the school of philosophy called logical positivism to the English-speaking world, was also known as an adamant atheist who "was so persuasive in his arguments, the story goes, that when the English writer Somerset Maugham lay dying, he got Sir Alfred to visit him and reassure him that there was no life after death." But in 1988, when Ayers' heart stopped for four minutes, "he wrote later that he had seen a red light and became 'aware that this light was responsible for the government of the universe.' The experience left his atheism unquenched ... but 'slightly weakened my conviction that my genuine death — which is due fairly soon — will be the end of me, though I continue to hope it will be.' "[7]

Jo and I edit an online newsletter for CSS Publishing called StoryShare, in which we share both short stories, parable-like stories, and "really happened" experiences of the Holy. We have received accounts of visions from all around the world. After one of the first issues, in December of 2002, a pastor wrote that he had seen a vision of Jesus in a parking lot of a carpet store after a Maundy Thursday service, as he was contemplating what he would preach on Good Friday. He said he didn't speak of it for eighteen months, until he found someone he could trust. He said he later

15

shared it with his congregation, but regretted it because people said things like, "What did he look like?" and "Why don't those things happen to me?" His conclusion was that he felt blessed by the encounter and needed that message from Jesus because of something he was struggling with, but that it was of no further use to anyone, so he doesn't share it anymore. But he wrote, "When I think of it, I tear up and get emotional, still these many years later."

Visions are not rare in our day, but there are many, like Samuel, who are afraid to tell what they see and hear. Eli convinces Samuel to tell him the whole thing, though in his case he knew it was not good news. Indeed, without the guidance of Eli, who in many other ways was a failure as a father and a priest, and was about to see his line of priests wiped out forever, Samuel might never have figured out who was calling his name. The instruction, the nurture, and the affirmation of the faith community is crucial to all who have visions. Without their willingness to hear and help in interpreting, many children, youth, and adults are left feeling very much alone. Dorothee Soelle writes: "Mystical experience is bliss and simultaneously it makes one homeless."[8]

1. Elizabeth Barrett Browning, from "Aurora Leigh," *The Treasury of Religious Verse*, compiler Donald T. Kauffman (Westwood: Fleming H. Revell Co., 1962), p. 11.

2. *The Messenger: The Story of Joan of Arc*, director Luc Besson, with Milla Jovovich, John Malkovich, Faye Dunaway, and Dustin Hoffman, Columbia Pictures, 1999.

3. Marcus Borg, *The God We Never Knew* (San Francisco: HarperCollins, 1997), p. 53.

4. Dorothee Soelle, *The Silent Cry: Mysticism and Resistance* (Minneapolis: Fortress Press, 2001), pp. 195-196.

5. William Johnston, *Arise My Love: Mysticism For A New Era* (Maryknoll: Orbis Books, 2000), p. 138.

6. Brad Steiger, *Revelation, The Divine Fire* (Englewood Cliffs; Prentice Hall, Inc., 1973), p. 14.

7. Eric Pace, *The New York Times*, Obituaries, 29 June, 1989.

8. Soelle, p. 196.

Advent

And then the presences — one or both of them, I do not know — spoke. This I heard clearly. Not in an ordinary way, for I cannot remember anything about the voice. But the message was beyond mistaking: "Everything is ready now."

Richard John Neuhaus

Richard John Neuhaus, *As I Lay Dying: Meditations Upon Returning* (New York: Basic Books, 2002), pp. 112-113.

The Voice Of The Broken Branch

Richard Whitaker

In those days and at that time I will cause a righteous Branch to spring up for David; and he shall execute justice and righteousness in the land. (v. 15)

Do not remember the sins of my youth or my transgressions; according to your steadfast love remember me, for your goodness' sake, O Lord! (v. 7)

In anger and bitterness, and with a stubborn tenacity to cling to what once had been in my life but was no more, at age fourteen I became a church "dropout." For six years I wandered in the wilderness, with God being rejected and pushed out of my life.

Then one day, when I was a sophomore at Georgia State College in Atlanta, I was approached by one of those Bible-thumping, tract-reading Campus Crusade for Christ guys. He invited me to a weekend retreat that just happened to be at North Georgia's Camp Glisson, where I had gone on several occasions as a child. Perhaps the retreat location convinced me to go along — I'm really not sure of my reasons for saying yes, but I agreed. Time has erased all memory of the weekend's theme, the speaker's name, or who else might have been there that I might have known. After the opening session on Friday evening, our speaker said to leave in silence and reflect for a few moments alone on the evening's message. It was a moonless, chilly October night, but I spotted a large tree near the baseball field that I targeted to become my quiet spot. As I hurried to the tree, which might partially insulate me from the enveloping cold, I stepped on something hard, which resulted in a loud cracking noise. It startled me and I looked at the ground beneath my feet. I discovered I had stepped on a very long and brittle tree branch that had broken completely in two. As I stopped to pick up the two pieces, that's when it happened.

A voice clearly spoke these words to me, not once, not twice, but over and over repeatedly, as a mantra, "My body, broken for you. My body, broken for you. My body, broken for you." I was immobile and speechless. Now shaking from cold, I began to weep. I crumpled into a heap against that tree, my eyes transfixed upon that broken tree limb now held in my hands. In that moment God's grace was made known to me and all I could do was weep. The tears kept flowing for what seemed a long, long time. I knew that Jesus had spoken my name, reminding me that although I had abandoned God, God had not forsaken me, and the sacrifice of Jesus had redeemed me from sin. Those childhood seeds from Sunday school *had* taken root. I remembered that Jesus' broken body on the cross had been given for my sins of indifference, anger, hurt, bitterness, and all the rest I had carried for six long years. I felt great remorse, yet a sense of inner healing. I also became aware that I was no longer physically cold.

The remaining part of that weekend is a completely empty picture, but a follow-up one-to-one sharing with this new Crusade brother in Christ several days later presented the challenge. He said, "So, the door has been opened by God, what will you do about it?" One month later, I opened a phone book's yellow pages and discovered the first United Methodist Church that was listed was the Avondale UMC, not far from where I lived. I made my way through those physical church doors the very next Sunday and in so doing I accepted Jesus' invitation to "come home." It was through this warm, welcoming, and forgiving congregation that God prepared me for a change in my career path which would lead me into becoming a full-time Christian educator. The "Voice of the Broken Branch" has been my sustenance throughout my lifelong spiritual journey. Thanks be to God that "his body was broken for me."

A Tender Mercy

Jenee Woodward

*"... By the tender mercy of our God, the dawn from
on high will break upon us, to give light to those
who sit in darkness and in the shadow of death, to
guide our feet into the way of peace."* (vv. 78-79)

Our son Phil has autism. He is ten years old and is severely
handicapped by his disability. Our family learned to slow down at
Christmas a number of years ago, when he was unable to tolerate
any of the celebration. He could not handle the changing scenarios
— the twinkling lights, the changes in grocery store displays, the
changes in the sanctuary at church, presents appearing under the
tree, the tree *itself*, and the moved furniture. He would fall down on
the floor and scream, unable to move, afraid to open his eyes, almost
constantly from Thanksgiving until well after Christmas, when it
was all over. We carried him through that time, his head covered
with his coat, so we could get through our daily errands, or sat with
him, huddled in his room, carefully ordered in *exactly* the same way
it had been since summer, with *no* Christmas trappings.

Of course our neighbor across the street is one of those folks
who buys every new outdoor Christmas display. Our son slept on
the sofa in the living room for two Decembers, trying to stay awake
so he could make sure that all of the lights across the street — on
the whole block! — were functioning correctly. If any went out, or
even when the lights came on or turned off outside at the proper
times, he would scream and cry in panic until they were fixed. Yes,
I spent an hour one cold night, on top of the neighbor's garage,
replacing *one bulb* in the Santa display so the boy would sleep!

Worship on Christmas Eve or Christmas Day was overcrowded
and yet hushed, not a good combination for an autistic child. Christmas celebrations at home were a nightmare. Phil would scream

and cry as each package was moved and (gasp!) unwrapped. As frightened as he was when each package appeared beneath the tree, he was equally frightened when it was removed from there or changed in the unwrapping process. We tried to find him a present he'd enjoy, but he'd merely scream and cry in panic at the intrusion on his carefully-ordered world, and the gifts would sit ignored until he outgrew them and we gave them to some little boy who could appreciate them.

He wanted nothing. He would look straight at toys we thought he would like, and he would not react at all. He asked for nothing. He anticipated nothing. He just screamed and cried at all of it. It is no bliss to have a child who doesn't get it — who doesn't want anything and doesn't want to have anything to do with Christmas commercialism. Or, it is only bliss in some romantic fantasy. In real life, it is a surreal nightmare.

This year, right around Thanksgiving, we once more asked the kids what they wanted for Christmas. Our fourteen-year-old daughter sat down and made out her list. And our ten-year-old son, for the first time in his life, answered the question. "PlayStation 2," he said. "I want PlayStation 2 Christmas." We just about fell over. His sister gave him a piece of paper. She wrote, "Phil's Christmas List" at the top. He wrote, "PLAYSTATION TOW" under her heading. "At Sam's," he said. "Go to car."

So, we drove to Sam's. Phil has never looked at anything there, never seemed to notice that Sam's has anything he might want. But he led us right to the PlayStation 2 sets, picked out the bundle he wanted and put it in the cart. "Open at Christmas," he said. He watched gleefully as we wrapped the package, and then he solemnly placed it under the tree. So, a PlayStation 2 game set sits there, wrapped, with his name on it, and he waits to open it. "December 25," he says. "Open PlayStation 2 December 25."

Last night, after we had returned from yet another Christmas rehearsal with our daughter, Phil found a *Best Buy* ad in the paper and turned immediately to the PlayStation games. He circled *Harry Potter* and *John Madden Football,* handed the ad to his father, and said, "I want Christmas." There were tears in my eyes. It's such a small thing, but such a truly amazing thing. It's one more bit of hope that he will be able to function in some semblance of society as an adult one day: that he might be able to live just a *bit* more independently, and one day want the things he needs to survive enough to work for them. This is not a forgone conclusion with autistic folks, which makes them particularly unemployable, no matter what their intelligence is. Consumerism might be "the enemy," but a kid who understands none of it is only a hero in *Chicken Soup for the Soul* stories.

This Advent season, I am grateful for being able to appreciate what complexity and miracle is involved in such small, "selfish" acts as wanting something for Christmas and expressing those wants to another person. I'm grateful that my son is able to enjoy all of the commercial cultural trappings of the holiday this year instead of running from them, screaming. I'm grateful for the many ways Phil helps me to stop and look again, even at my most "Christian" conclusions. And I'm especially grateful that my son helps me see Christ's humble birth, over and over again, even in the midst of nightmares and worries I could not have imagined ten years ago, even in the midst of Advent.

Christmas Tears

Christinia Seibel

With joy you will draw water from the wells of salvation. And you will say in that day: Give thanks to the Lord, call on his name; make known his deeds among the nations; proclaim that his name is exalted. (vv. 3-4)

I think nothing breaks our hearts as badly as does the broken hearts of our children. My daughter, Melissa, moved back in with my husband and I just before Thanksgiving. Her husband had left her and wanted nothing to do with the baby they were expecting.

In the early morning hours of Christmas Eve Day, as the world prepared to celebrate the birth of the Babe of Bethlehem, I held my daughter's hand as she gave birth to a premature stillborn child, due to a separated placenta. Baby Afton Long was born and died on Christmas Eve Day.

As I held my stillborn grandchild, my daughter, with a broken heart and tear-filled eyes, looked up at me and said, "Mom, I know we can't baptize the baby — but can you give my baby a blessing?" As she named her baby, we prayed together. Then she held her baby so tenderly, marveling at how perfectly formed the baby was: ten toes, ten fingers. Through it all, a song from the Christmas Eve cantata kept echoing in my mind. "Be Exalted, O God."

Yet, in the midst of great tragedy, there were tears of joy.

After notifying family members by phone, my father's closing words to me were, "Remember, Christmas still happens. Christ still comes." He was so right. God's abundant grace has indeed been with us.

The hospital staff and Melissa's obstetrician were truly God's hands of compassion that night. They were wonderful. The Senior Pastor at the church, where my husband (who is my daughter's stepfather, as her dad died six years ago) serves as Associate Pastor, offered to let my husband preach at my Christmas Eve services, so that I could continue to be with my daughter. It gave us precious time together to cry, to pray, and for me just to sit and hold her while she cried and slept. So many people — friends, family, church members — have offered their prayers and condolences. It got us through the first night. Then, Christmas morning, my council president and his fiancée called to say that Christmas dinner was being provided. Later on, a homemade "with all the trimmings" Christmas dinner was delivered to our door.

And then, Christmas night, as I helped my daughter get into bed, she hugged me and said through her tears, "Mom, it's so much harder at night. I love you so much! Thanks for everything. I don't know what I would have done without you." Then she looked up at me and said, "I don't mean this to sound weird, but I have really been feeling God's presence in this." The cantata hymn rang out in my mind once again, "Be Exalted, O God!"

I give thanks to God for the grace that has sustained my daughter thus far. And I know she has a long road to go yet, so please, pray for Melissa, for healing from grief, for healing from surgery, and for healing from a broken marriage.

The Christmas Tree:
A Story Of Synchronicity

Jane Moschenrose

He has brought down the powerful from their thrones, and lifted up the lowly; he has filled the hungry with good things, and sent the rich away empty. (vv. 52-53)

It was a week before Christmas. Both my husband and I are pastors, at different churches, and life was hectic. My family had agreed not to get a Christmas tree this year, because our schedules didn't allow us to enjoy it anyway, and we would be gone on vacation beginning on Christmas Day.

But for some reason my eyes were drawn to the ad on my church's bulletin board for the Lion's Club Christmas Tree Sale every time I passed it in the hall. Finally, on December 23, I gave in and went down the street to the sale. I introduced myself to the volunteer Lion's Club member at the cash register and confessed my inability to get his sale out of my mind. He sat up straight, with an excited look on his face. "Oh, do you know of a family who could use our help? We usually take care of Christmas for a couple of families a year. We get gifts for everybody in the family, a Christmas tree, food basket, the whole thing. But this year we just couldn't get the cooperation from the town. They didn't give us any names. Do you know anybody?"

A family from the community, who probably hadn't sought or received any help, came to mind. They were very independent, private people, and worked hard to support their four children. The past year, though, had been full of illness for both of the parents, and there was nothing extra for a Christmas celebration. I gave the Lion's Club member their name and address, took a tree home, and thought nothing more of it.

A couple of weeks later, my husband happened to run into the mother of this family. As it turns out, during the week before Christmas she had been having an extremely difficult time, to the point where she felt everyone would be better off without her. On the very night she planned to commit suicide, the doorbell rang. The Lion's Club came in with Christmas for the family.

She told my husband, "I knew then that God was watching out for us, and we would make it through this rough time."

Was it a coincidence that I was oddly drawn to that ad for the Christmas Tree Sale at the very time the salesperson was seeking a family to help, and the family I thought of to help happened to include a person who needed hope and faith restored? Or was this the active hand of God, granting this woman hope during a time of hopelessness? I vote for the latter.

Christmas

From infancy you have been taught, not bodily but spiritually, by true vision through the Spirit of the Lord. Speak these things that you now see and hear ... speak and write, therefore, now according to me and not according to yourself.

Hildegard of Bingen

Hildegard of Bingen, *The Book of the Rewards of Life,* trans. Bruce W. Hozeski (New York: Oxford University Press, 1994), pp. 9-10.

An Unlikely Angel

David Michael Smith

*Then an angel of the Lord stood before them, and
the glory of the Lord shone around them, and they
were terrified.* (v. 9)

He staggered in fifteen minutes after the traditional holiday
hymn sing had begun, plopping with a thud in the wooden pew
directly behind me. It was Christmas Eve night at historic St. Paul's
Episcopal Church in the small and quaint town of Georgetown,
Delaware, and midnight mass was scheduled to commence in about
twenty minutes. Dozens of candles cast a warm glow throughout
the church. The pipe organist was playing a seasonal tune, the congregation joining the choir in a unified voice of celebration and
joy.

I recall smelling the strong odor of alcohol, right behind me.
Trying to appear inconspicuous, I nonchalantly turned at an angle
while still pretending to sing so I could glance at the whiskey-
breathed intruder. A young man, perhaps age 25, maybe younger,
sat alone in the pew, a drunken smile plastered across his unshaven
face. His hair was bushy and uncombed, his clothing unbefitting of
a holy and reverent church service. I did not recognize the fellow,
and later would learn that nobody else knew who the man was
either. And Georgetown's the type of friendly place where everyone seems to know just about everyone else, and their family tree.
Just call us "Mayberry."

It became immediately obvious to me that the man was confused, disoriented. Not just with the Christmas Eve service, which
for a first-time visitor can be somewhat perplexing despite the bul-
letins the ushers hand out, but in general. He stumbled aimlessly
through the hymnal and a prayer book like a child leafing through
coloring books at the doctor's office. He was intoxicated and his

behavior made me uncomfortable. Judging by the numerous nervous stares I observed, targeted in the young man's direction, some subtle and some not so subtle, others shared my opinion.

Then, a good-natured parishioner named Bob left his family and his regularly-appointed pew, and joined the fellow, shaking his hand and introducing himself with a warm smile. Bob helped the man throughout the remainder of the hymn sing, assisting the delighted guy with locating the proper songs and directing him with basic liturgical functions such as when to stand, sit, and kneel. With each song, the intoxicated stranger sang zealously louder and genuinely off key, although I suspect he felt he was performing as well as Pavarotti or Sinatra. I found his butchering of the traditional holiday carols both disturbing and amusing at the same time. He was having enthusiastic fun. But he surely couldn't sing a lick! Indeed, our uninvited visitor was certainly a ball of tightly-bound entertainment. The hymn sing-a-long ended and the service began with "O Come, All Ye Faithful," a procession of priests in robes and acolytes bearing torches entering from the back of the church. Someone in the procession waved a canister of incense around, preparing the sanctuary for worship and God's presence, but it made my eyes water and I sneezed. The service continued without incident with prayer and Bible readings about the birth of the Savior, the infant Jesus. Good Samaritan Bob continued to befriend the man, much to his delight. I traded smiles with the man, my heart softening.

"Why was I angry that he came here tonight?" I thought to myself. "This is God's house, not mine, and all are welcomed in the Lord's house." I wondered if the young man was lonely, depressed on this wonderful holiday eve, first seeking the comfort of a bottle, drowning unknown sorrows, and later journeying by our church. Perhaps he heard the festive Christmas music outside the ancient brick walls, and then saw the church aglow, holly wreaths hanging from the huge oaken doors, like one of those wonderful Thomas Kinkade paintings, so inviting. Something deep within his heart led him to come inside, an inner voice urging him to enter the warmth of the real-life artwork. Maybe he was simply in need of acceptance and love. I pondered about who he was and where he was from. Did he have a family? Was he married? Children? He was somebody.

Then, the priest moved to the pulpit to begin his Christmas homily. The Father had preached for only a few minutes when abruptly he stopped his sermon message. I thought he had lost his place, or was pausing for oratorical effect. But I was wrong. I noticed him looking down on the congregation, a concerned frown rippling across his forehead. A low, curious murmur spread throughout the people. About four pews back from the front, on the left side, often referred to as the Epistle side, Bill, an elderly man who faithfully attended each and every Sunday, had slumped over. Several members of the congregation moved to his aid, thinking he had merely passed out. The situation, however, was far graver.

The service came to a complete halt as one parishioner sprinted to call 9-1-1. Several people laid Bill down on his back in the pew and attempted to revive him. Although there were several full-time nurses on hand this evening and a medical doctor by trade, the matter did not appear good. Bill was unconscious and had stopped breathing, and his pulse was weak. Even from across the center aisle in dim lighting I could see his flesh turning gray. The oddest feeling ran through me.

Stunned, most of us just sat or stood in our pews, paralyzed with fear and disbelief. A beloved man of our church community was dying before our very eyes, and suddenly it no longer felt like Christmas Eve. I felt helpless, lost. Then a voice spoke out.

"Why don't we all get down on our knees and pray for the old guy?" the voice bellowed from behind me. It was our visitor, his voice slurred, but strong. "Maybe God can help him."

Like a slap in the face, many of us snapped out of our panicked stupor and knelt in agreement with the man's suggestion. There was no debate, only silent obedience to the idea. As several people continued to tend to Bill, who was near death, the rest of the congregation prayed in honest, pleading whispers. I prayed harder and more sincerely than I ever had, my wet eyes tightly shut.

Moments later, I heard a commotion to my left. I opened my eyes just as I whispered "Amen," and was shocked to see Bill sitting up, his eyes open, the paleness in his face rapidly disappearing.

Happy sobs could be heard throughout the church, our prayers gloriously answered! Despite numerous inquiries, Bill determinedly assured us that he was fine. When the paramedics arrived, racing down the center aisle with their equipment and stretcher, he refused to go to the hospital with them, insisting on staying for the conclusion of the Christmas Eve mass. And after everything settled down, the service was in fact finished without further incident.

After the closing benediction and song, a raucous "Joy To The World," I turned to shake the young man's hand, but he was gone. He apparently had left during the Eucharist as the congregation filed pew-by-pew for the bread and wine, the body and blood of our Savior.

Later, I discovered that no one had ever seen the man leave. It was as if he simply vanished into thin air. No one knew his identity or anything about him. He was no one's relative, or neighbor, or co-worker. Who was the man that visited us on that precious, special night, a night we each witnessed a true miracle? A dying man was revived, saved from death, neither by science nor medicine, but by faithful prayer to God in heaven. Prayer initiated by a common stranger, a person like you or me perhaps, or the guy we pass every day in the street and pay no attention to, an unlikely angel.

A Christmas Story From Cambodia

Patricia Lyon

For the grace of God has appeared, bringing sal-
vation to all, training us to renounce impiety and
worldly passions, and in the present age to live
lives that are self-controlled, upright, and godly....
(vv. 11-12)

I wondered if the village folk ever had potlucks like the Methodists back home. So I asked Mara, "Do you ever have parties where everyone brings some food?"

"Oh, no, Madame," he said. "Maybe at Christmas we have party for Jesus." The next day, he brought me a picture of how the church was decorated for Christmas. The "Christmas Tree" was a kind of fern bush propped up against the corner of the church. I had seen the fern bushes growing about fifteen kilometers away, near the dam we had visited. They were odd-looking, prehistoric kinds of plants that vaguely resembled a white pine. The "needles" were the fronds of the palms.

"What is on the Christmas tree?" I asked my co-teacher.

"That snow, Madame." I recognized some stretched-out, pathetic looking cosmetic cotton balls.

"Cambodian Christmas different from United States," I thought.

Today I am overwhelmed with the possibilities of buying, looking, baking, eating, watching, and doing for Christmas. I can get tired just thinking about it. I remember a warmer place, where people have simple ideas about Christmas. My Cambodian friends won't shop. They won't have electric lights. They won't have cookies. No stockings to hang. It doesn't matter; there are no chimneys. Hardly anyone knows who Mickey Mouse is, so I am not sure they know about the Jolly Old Elf and his eight tiny reindeer. The Grinch has not been to the village.

When I find myself getting stressed out over the things I think I must do to "have" Christmas, I will try to remember there is another way. In Cambodia, Christmas will be like any other day, except for three percent of the population who are Christians. It will be okay if Christmas is not white. Somehow they will find a way to show their love for each other without presents. Rice will substitute for "Figgy Pudding." They will understand that the Savior has no place to live because that is their story, too. No one will have to wish them a "Merry Little Christmas." It will be little and merry, anyway.

Saved

Cheryl Kirking

Bear with one another and, if anyone has a complaint against another, forgive each other; just as the Lord has forgiven you, so you also must forgive. Above all, clothe yourselves with love, which binds everything together in perfect harmony. (vv. 11-12)

"I may have a story for your book, Cheryl." I had just finished presenting at a women's event, and had told the audience that I was compiling this book of Christmas stories. She had been lingering near the table where I was signing books, and I could see she wanted to wait until the crowd had dwindled.

She was in her mid-sixties, trim and attractive, with perfectly-coiffed silver hair and wearing a stylish navy pantsuit. I smiled enthusiastically. "Well, great! Tell me!" I urged.

"No. There are so many women who still want to speak to you — I don't want to monopolize your time." She leaned close, almost whispering. "When you're done here, could you meet with me in the lounge by the library? It won't take long."

"Okay!" I whispered back with a smile.

After greeting the few remaining women, I left my husband, who had traveled with me, to pack our sound equipment. I wandered down the deserted hallways to the library lounge where she was waiting, as promised.

"Hi!" I smiled, extending my hand. "I'm sorry. I didn't catch your name...?"

"It's Joanna," she smiled back, squeezing my hand. "I appreciate your staying late ... I know you must be tired. But I didn't want to take you away from the others. And ..." she glanced at the door, "I really don't want anyone to overhear."

We sat on the couch. She smoothed her slacks and examined her manicured nails. Looking up, she smiled. "After I tell you my story, you'll understand why I don't want anyone to overhear."

I nodded, trying my best to look understanding.

"Well," she began with a sign. "I've never told anyone this, but I have wanted to. It's not something I'm proud of, but, in a strange way, I'm glad it happened."

I nodded again, my curiosity piqued.

"It happened almost thirty years ago, in mid-December. It was three days before my husband's company Christmas party. I was doing a little shopping, and feeling sorry for myself, I guess. I couldn't buy the cocktail dress I wanted, and would wear an 'old' dress to the party instead. My husband owned his own company then, and business had not been good that year. He felt like a failure, and I was frustrated that he had given all the employees a raise the year before, and yet we were struggling to maintain our current lifestyle. And our lifestyle was a struggle to maintain even in a good year." She smiled wryly. "We tend to live *far* beyond our means."

"Well," she continued, "as I was Christmas shopping I thought I'd take a peek at the jewelry counter, and I spotted a gold cloisonné bangle bracelet. Not solid gold, probably gold-plated, but with a lovely enameled design. It wasn't terribly expensive, maybe thirty dollars. I certainly didn't need it. But I *felt* like I *needed* it — needed something new, just for *me*. I don't know how else to explain it. I just felt that I *deserved* that bracelet!

"And ... Cheryl," she looked at me intensely. "I *took* the bracelet! Just slipped it on, and went about my shopping. I almost ... *almost* ... left the store with it on. The voice inside me kept saying, 'Joanna, this isn't like you! It isn't right!' But I kept it on, until my conscience got the better of me and I decided to put it back. As I was hanging it back on the display rack, I jumped at the sound of a man's voice. 'So, you decided against the bracelet?' A man in a brown jacket was suddenly standing right next to me. My nerves were completely rattled, but I tried to appear nonchalant as I asked, 'I beg your pardon?' And he answered, 'I noticed you putting that bracelet back.'

"I tried to sound innocent, but I was stammering, 'Yes, well ... I had tried it on, you see ... and I forgot I was wearing it.' He gave me this look, this incriminating look, and said, 'Uh huh ... well, I'm glad you remembered to put it back.'

"I was *furious* at his insinuation! Oh, I was indignant! As I turned to storm away, he repeated, '*Really*, ma'am, I'm *really* glad you decided to put it back.' This time his voice was soft ... forgiving. It was like he was looking directly into my soul.

"He must have worked for the store's security. He must have seen me take it! I was that close to being arrested for shoplifting!" She held her thumb and forefinger a quarter-inch apart. "And for what? A little bracelet!

"I don't even remember driving home, but when I got there, I just fell through the kitchen doorway and collapsed onto the floor. Just crumbled, my forehead on the floor, and kept saying 'Oh god, oh god, oh god.' Thinking over and over how I could have been arrested, how my reputation would have been ruined, how stupid I was, how *angry* I was at that security guy ... and at myself. I was just shaking, shivering, repeating in disbelief. 'Oh god, oh god, oh god!'

"Then after five, maybe ten, minutes — my words took on a different tone. 'Oh, *God*!' My words became a cry to the Almighty. 'Oh, God! Oh, God! Oh, *God*!' I was crying out for forgiveness, asking him to help erase my haughtiness, begging him to come and fill the void that I foolishly thought a new dress and jewelry might fill. But I think I knew, deep down, it wasn't about the bracelet. It was about so, so much *more* that was missing in my life! I promised him I'd change. I asked *him to change me*. I was so ashamed, and yet ... an incredible feeling of relief flooded over me. I knew that I was *forgiven*. Forgiven, not just for the bracelet incident, but for *all* my sins. My cry became words of humility and gratitude. Words of praise! 'Oh, *God*! Oh, *God*! Oh, *God*!'

"So ..." she sighed, dropping her hands on her lap. "That's my Christmas story ... not just because it happened at Christmastime, but because it's when Jesus came to me, like he came to the world at Christmas."

"Or maybe the day you came to *him*," I pondered quietly.

"Yes! Yes — that's exactly how it was!" she exclaimed. "I came to him and made a promise, and accepted his promise. He saved me from ... myself. Saved me from an empty life. I am so much more ..." She searched for the word. "So much more ... *compassionate* now. I realize that my weaknesses are no less sinful than those of others who have more 'obvious' faults. I'm not proud of my story, but I think it has a purpose. I don't know what you might want to do with it, but if you think it might help somebody, you can use it however you wish. Maybe you can find a way to make it seem ... interesting."

"Oh, I think it's plenty interesting, Joanna," I said, giving her a hug. "And thank you for sharing your story. I know it will touch people's hearts."

It had already touched mine. It reminded me that we have a great God, who *so loved the world that he gave his only begotten son.* A Savior who came to us as a humble baby. Accessible, that we might come to him, to receive his promise: of forgiveness, of love, of eternity. Who hears us when we humbly cry out, *"Oh, God!"*

> *"If my people, who are called by my name, humble themselves and pray and seek my face and turn from their wicked ways, then will I hear from heaven and will forgive their sin and will heal their land ... Now my eyes will be open and my ears attentive to the prayers offered ... my eyes and my heart will always be there."*
> — 2 Chronicles 7:14-16 (paraphrased)

"Saved" is originally printed in the book *All is Calm, All is Bright: True Stories of Christmas*, by Cheryl Kirking (Fleming H. Revell Publishers ©2001). Visit her website at www.cherylkirking.com.

He Will Wipe Away Every Tear

Rosmarie Trapp

And I heard a loud voice from the throne saying, "See, the home of God is among mortals. He will dwell with them as their God; they will be his peoples, and God himself will be with them; he will wipe every tear from their eyes. Death will be no more; mourning and crying and pain will be no more, for the first things have passed away."
(vv. 3-4)

In 1987, I came to Stowe, Vermont, for a visit with my mother, Maria Von Trapp. Her maid met us at the door with the news that mother was very ill and the ambulance was coming to take her to the hospital. Her friend, Emily Johnson, and I followed, and I had to sign a permission form for an exploratory surgery, as no other members of the family were available. My family was scattered in Europe, Arizona, Maryland, and elsewhere.

It was my mother's custom to bless us with a cross on the forehead. After a kiss, that was the last thing she did for me, as she never came out of the anesthesia. Her body was too deteriorated for them to operate. She was in a coma for three days.

The family gathered, friends came, we had mass said in the ICU bedroom with her, and we sang lots of our family songs for her. At her actual passing, only my younger sister, Lorli, and my niece, Elisabeth, were there. Werner, my older brother, his wife, Fr. Paul Taggart, and I were having dinner at the Trapp Lodge. Tina, the harpist, was playing "In the Garden," a favorite of my mother's, when the message came of her passing. It made Werner cry, for he felt it was a sign from mother that she was in the garden of Paradise. My request to God was that she would see somebody from heaven come to meet her, and she did, for we were told she opened her eyes and sat up in joyful greeting just before she died. It makes me cry just to write this, but oh, the comfort!

Many years later, our pastor in Pittsburgh, Pennsylvania, Eddie Donovan, told me of a dream he had: He was walking through paradise and came on my mother, Maria, and her friend, Emily, sitting on a bench reading poetry. He asked if he could sit with them, but they told him the grass would do, as the bench was small. So he sat at their feet and listened. What a dream, again, so comforting! Three signs for me to be sure she was there, and someday I'll be there, too, God willing. And we'll get along better than we ever did on earth!

Editor's Note: Rosmarie von Trapp is the daughter of Captain George and Maria von Trapp whose story was told in the movie, *The Sound of Music*. Rosmarie was the first of three children born to the von Trapps after their marriage. The widowed captain already had seven children when Maria came to be the family governess. Rosmarie and her nine brothers and sisters made up the von Trapp Family singers who became famous after their triumphant flight from Nazi-controlled Austria in the 1930s.

Epiphany

"Strike me down dead if they's a God!" Tom yelled
... we waited. Then a little whirlwind came along
the hillside, rattling the dead oak leaves, seeming
to attack one tree at a time. It took hold of the tree
where we stood, thrashed with it, filling the woods
with sound.

Ben Logan

Ben Logan, *The Land Remembers: The Story of A Farm and
Its People* (Minnetonka: Northword Press, 1999), pp. 205-206.

Seeing The Light

Arise, shine; for your light has come, and the glory
of the Lord has risen upon you. For darkness shall
cover the earth, and thick darkness the peoples;
but the Lord will arise upon you, and his glory
will appear over you. (vv. 1-2)

Timothy Paulson, as told to Robert Gossett

Much of my Christian experience has come through the "School of Hard Knocks," better known as prison. I was raised in church and Sunday school, but God wasn't very important to me in my younger years. Alcohol and other drugs seemed to offer much more fun and excitement than thinking about God. It was that combination, along with my jealousy and temper, that resulted in a two-and-a-half-year stay in the Wisconsin state prison system following abuse of my wife and fighting with the police who came to investigate. I knew that I deserved the sentence I eventually received, but I was embarrassed by what people would think and upset that I would not be very much involved in my children's lives while I was in prison.

When my pastor heard about my problems, he invited me to attend a prayer group that had started at the church. I began to attend, knowing I would need all the prayer I could get in the months and years ahead. My relationship with God began to grow at that point, and continued during my stay in prison through my personal Bible study and participation in study groups. My local church supported me with prayer and letters, and I began to believe that my life was worth something.

As my faith grew, I hungered for an even deeper experience of God. One night, while fasting, I skipped supper and spent about twenty minutes kneeling by my bunk in prayer. I cried out, "Lord, reveal yourself! I really want to know you." Suddenly a light, brighter than anything I had ever seen before, surrounded me. A tingling sensation went through my body and I knew that God had touched me deeply. I was filled with God's joy and peace. When my cellmate returned from supper, he said, "Tim, what in the world happened to you?" I told him and he couldn't wait to get out of the room. The guards and other inmates could see the difference as well. Some were happy for me and others just waited for me to fall.

What difference has this made in my life? The joy and peace remained during the rest of my time in prison and since I've returned home. I often marvel at it, because of what I continue to go through with embarrassment about being an ex-con, financial and health problems, family concerns, and much more. God has also delivered me from any desire for alcohol and other drugs. The joy I find in the Lord is much greater than anything I thought I was finding in those things that I had used in dealing with life. I realize there are still people who are waiting for me to fall, but there are many more who are there to love me and support me in spite of my past failures.

My desire is to use my past mistakes to help others who may be in similar situations. I want to continue to grow in my faith and use it in obedience, wherever God may lead. I'm glad I'm where I am in my faith and life, even if it took a difficult lesson in the School of Hard Knocks to get there.

David E. Cobb

"Daddy, I saw the star of Bethlehem!" That's how I woke up on the Thursday after Epiphany. My four-and-a-half-year-old son, Jackson, was standing next to my pillow announcing excitedly that he had seen the star of Bethlehem in the east. He was really jazzed. Katy and I quickly got out of bed and went straight to his bedroom window. The sun had not yet risen. We looked up, through the tree branches into the sky, and sure enough, there in the east was a bright light, larger than any star or planet I'd ever seen, not moving or flashing like an airplane, but enormous. "Let's go out-side," I said. I grabbed the binoculars from the closet, and Jackson and I stepped out into the chilly pre-dawn air. It was still there. Katy followed. The three of us took turns looking through the binoculars, amazed at the size and brilliance of it. I wished I had a telescope.

We haven't told him yet that it was probably Jupiter. At least that's what the newspaper said we'd find in the pre-dawn eastern sky. For Jackson, just a few days after Epiphany and the visitation of the magi, he knew what it was. Standing there in his pajamas and slippers, he said, "Let's follow it so we can find Jesus."

I think I said something like, "That was a long time ago, and Bethlehem is very far away. Maybe this star is telling us to look for Jesus here where we live."

He looked up at me and said, "That's okay, Daddy. I'll find him."

Perhaps he already has.

Remember Your Baptism

Theonia Amenda

*Now when all the people were baptized, and when
Jesus also had been baptized and was praying, the
heaven was opened, and the Holy Spirit descended
upon him in bodily form like a dove. And a voice
came from heaven, "You are my Son, the Beloved;
with you I am well pleased." (vv. 21-22)*

It was 1984. I was sitting in the front row in a classroom in
Nashville, listening to Dr. Bruce Rigdon speak on Orthodox Spirituality. He was sharing about a Greek Orthodox baptism on the isle
of Crete in which he participated as the godfather of Demetri, the
son of a close colleague.

The sacrament of baptism began at home, where Demetri was
scrubbed with a brush in soap and water, dressed, and then brought
to the church with his family. The ceremony and liturgy began outside the church doors where everyone gathered with the family
and priest. All were asked, "Why are you here?"

They responded by turning to the west and saying they were
called to renounce death, sin, and the demonic. Then, turning to
the east, the community pledged themselves in their responsibility
to help bring Demetri up as a member of the kingdom of Christ.
Then the priest knocked three times on the door to enter the sanctuary where the baptismal font was situated. In this little church, it
was a huge wooden scrub bucket.

The water was poured in by the ladies of that congregation,
making certain it was the right temperature for the infant, and then
the water was blessed by the priest. Demetri's clothes were removed and Demetri was dunked three times in the water and lifted
up three times as the priest proclaimed, above the child's protesting wails:

Demetri ... Child of God!
Demetri ... Child of God!
Demetri ... Child of God!

If the child had not screamed, they would have pinched him to make him cry, because the first thing one listens for in the trauma of natural birth is the cry of the child, that says, in essence, "Here I am ... alive!"

Then Demetri was dried and the royal robe was put on him, and he was taken to the front of the sanctuary to be presented to the icons. The Orthodox believe that the icons are the visible presence of the Lord and of all the saints, which they portray. The priest took him to the icon of Saint John and presented him as he said, "Blessed Saint John, Demetri, Child of God"; next to Saint Paul, "Blessed Saint Paul, Demetri, Child of God," and on to each of the icons, and then finally back to the gathered community, because the gathered community are also icons, who, along with us, also bear the image of God. And once more he said, "Brothers and Sisters in Christ, Demetri, Child of God."

Demetri had now entered a new loyalty. He had been scrubbed, cleaned, and purified. He had entered the death and resurrection of Christ. He belonged to a new family — the church — the body of Christ. Now that was a lot, but only the beginning.

In the early church, for centuries, three things were always kept together — baptism, anointing with oil, and the Lord's Supper. So the congregation, with the priest, offered prayers that the Holy Spirit would now descend upon this child and fill him and confirm his baptism, as it is the Spirit who confirms. And that promise of God was sealed by the making of the sign of the cross in holy oil on Demetri's forehead, hands, the back of his neck, and his feet. All symbolized that the gift of the Spirit was given to him and compels him to grow into a servant of God.

Then Demetri was taken to the altar, and together with the people of God, he celebrated the Lord's Supper, and was the first served. Demetri's mouth was opened to receive a spoon of wine with pieces of bread in it. From that moment on, Demetri was welcomed at the Lord's table so he could learn what it means to be a servant of Christ, just as we are invited to our earthly family's table where we learn what it means to be part of our families.

Well, the story of Demetri's baptism was one powerful story for this female! Bruce Rigdon had given me the gift of hearing, for the first time, the liturgy and meaning of my *own* baptism in the Greek Orthodox Church in Milwaukee when I was an infant.

I found tears were running down my face as I listened to the words that were pronounced at my own baptism: the words that claimed *me* as God's child. I had never heard them before. I hadn't even known that I needed to hear them, until that moment — to hear about the grace of God that was given to me forever, as well as the claim of God on my life.

When the lecture was over, a member of the community came up behind me to return some sun tanning oil he had borrowed, and held it playfully over my head, saying, "Theonia, I anoint you with oil," or something like that. He had no idea what I had experienced through this lecture. But the words started my sobbing, and my covenant group of seven saw what was happening and gathered around me in a huddle while the tears rolled out of my soul — tears of healing and of joy!

That night in our covenant group, after the sharing of the day and where we had heard God speaking to us, they said they wanted to do something for me after Night Prayer.

We went to Night Prayers in the Upper Room Chapel, where a life-size carving of Leonardo da Vinci's portrayal of the Last Supper hangs across the front. After everyone else had left, my covenant group took me up to the chancel, in front of the communion table, and told me to lie down on my back on the floor. The seven of them then proceeded to lift me up, above their heads, three times (which is no small feat!), as they said,

Theonia ... Child of God!
Theonia ... Child of God!
Theonia ... Child of God!

What a gift they gave me that night. More than the act itself, even, was their love and understanding of my life, and what hearing those words would mean to me. I didn't need to be rebaptized, but I certainly did need to remember my baptism and to claim again the power of the grace of my baptism — that no matter what, without any qualifiers, I was and always would be a Child of God — a daughter of God, accepted completely, always and forever: not needing to do a thing to earn it: just remember it, accept it, claim it, and live out of it ... the power and grace of my own baptism.

That was, and is, my true identity. That is *our* true identity, each of us, no matter what has happened in our lives. We all need to remember our baptisms every day of our lives: to remember who and whose we are — a child of God, loved unconditionally — to remember that grace of our baptism with thanksgiving. We are called not only to remember that, but to accept it, claim it, and live out of it! Amen.

You Save Humans And Animals Alike

Your righteousness is like the mighty mountains,
your judgments are like the great deep; you save
humans and animals alike, O Lord. (v. 6)

Wayne Frank

About four years ago, I was living alone in a big three-bedroom house on south Layton Boulevard on Milwaukee's south side. I was alone because I was divorced and although I had a girlfriend, or more accurately, a number of girlfriends, I preferred to live alone, with one exception — my little black mongrel dog, Muffy.

Muffy had been born in that house about fourteen years earlier. She was the runt of the litter, and either my wife or I frequently had to help her locate her mother's nipple in order for her to survive. We grew fond of her. Against my better judgment, I agreed to keep her, along with her mother, in the house. A few years later, my wife and I suffered through a painful divorce. Muffy's mother eventually had to be put to sleep in advanced old age, leaving Muffy and me alone. But we were buddies. Years passed. Muffy got older. She eventually went blind, lost all but two of her teeth, and then lost her hearing. When I came home I would pound on the walls so she could feel the vibrations throughout the house and know she was no longer alone, and come to the door to greet me. After a while she stopped coming to greet me and I had to carry her up from the basement for visits. She was confined to the basement because she was no longer capable of controlling herself. Still, I made a vow that as long as she was not in pain, I would take care of her with the hope that she might die peacefully at home. After all, she was my buddy. But it was not to be.

One day, I came home and could not find her in the basement. I looked seemingly everywhere. It was useless to shout. A second search found her in a dark corner, covered with cobwebs, staring vacantly at the wall. I knew she had been sitting like that for hours. I knew in an instant that it was the end; this was no longer a life, not any way to live for this little animal that had been my friend for so many years. I called the veterinarian to make arrangements for the next morning. I gave her a treat — three soft meat dishes to choose from for supper. That night I went to bed with a very heavy heart, because of the vow I had made versus reality. Then, sometime after falling asleep, I awoke suddenly, first feeling sadness and then joy. I had dreamt that Muffy had died and I was kneeling in front of her sad little carcass of black fur. In my dream I was terribly saddened by her death and I was crying, when, on my left, I saw what I think was either a man or an angel in a white robe. I did not see his face, because he slowly pointed with his right hand and my gaze followed his hand. I turned and saw a white female dog with seven or eight very young puppies, all excitedly feeding, tails wagging, happy, happy, happy, as only puppies can be. They were white like their mother. Remember, Muffy was black. For some unexplained reason, I called out Muffy's name and one of the white puppies on the right raised its head, turned, and looked right at me. I knew that white puppy was Muffy, and she had heard and recognized her name.

I believe God sent me a vision of understanding in that dream. He was telling me what would happen to Muffy, perhaps what happens to all of his animals. It was all right to let her go, to put her to sleep, despite my promise to her (and God), because right after death, she would become a puppy again and live a new life, and it was okay. Thank you, God. Thank you, Muffy.

Vanessa Bruce Ingold

A few months after I had become a Christian, I started going to Hollywood, with some friends from church, to tell people about Jesus and feed the homeless. First, we would meet at church and make bologna sandwiches. Then, since it was approximately a forty-minute drive, we'd carpool to Hollywood Boulevard. We would bring Christian pamphlets explaining our faith. Thus, we gave physical and spiritual food away as we walked down the boulevard.

One summer Saturday night, there were only four of us who had met to make sandwiches. We only had two loaves of bread, with just enough bologna to fill the two empty bags with sandwiches. We had been walking down the boulevard for twenty minutes. We stopped in front of a liquor store.

"Hey, guys, Vanessa and I are going inside the liquor store to get some gum," my friend Paul told the two others. They were holding the last few sandwiches.

"Okay," they said, as they were in a discussion with someone they had just met, who was asking them about our beliefs.

Now, with a package of Big Red gum, Paul and I stood at the counter. I turned to see a short, grubby, unshaven man walk into the store. The soles of his shoes were completely worn out, and the front of his shoes were so badly torn that all ten of his dirty toes could be seen. As he walked, his shoes looked like ducks' mouths flapping. I desperately wanted to get him some food. I stuck my hands in my pockets; nope, I was penniless.

"Paul," I said, turning to him, "do you have a few dollars; or some change at least?"

"No," he replied. He had used his last few cents to buy the Big Red. "But, let's go see if they've got some sandwiches left."

I walked up to the homeless man and asked him if he wanted some food. He eagerly nodded his head up and down and followed us outside. Although it was getting dark, and becoming more crowded and noisy down the famous boulevard, we located our two friends. As we approached them, Paul loudly asked, "Do you guys have any more sandwiches?"

Before they could say no, "Bread," was the only word spoken by a passing young woman who flung her hand forward, holding a full loaf of fresh bread. The man grabbed hold of it. The woman's hand seemingly disappeared. Surprised by the spontaneous and quick transaction, I tried to trace her with my eyes; however, she camouflaged in with the moving crowd.

The almost toothless man held the bread, smiling. "All right!" my three buddies said, congratulating him, as they patted him on the back.

"Do you think she was an angel?" I asked the three of them, as the grinning man went on his way. We all agreed that we won't know until we're in Heaven. When I think of that today, I am still amazed at how God provided when I had nothing to give.

The Call Of God

*And he rolled up the scroll, gave it back to the
attendant, and sat down. The eyes of all in the syna-
gogue were fixed on him. Then he began to say to
them, "Today this scripture has been fulfilled in
your hearing." (vv. 20-21)*

Roy Nelson

I had been struggling with the call to the ordained ministry for
several years. I knew God was calling, but I didn't really want to
go. After all, I had a wife and two young children to support, I had
a great job that I really enjoyed, and I was active in men's ministry
at my church. Why couldn't God be happy with what I was doing
in ministry as a layperson? Why couldn't he just leave me where I
was? It was nice. It was good. It was, well, comfortable.

I felt as though God was really on my back. The weight of
knowing he wanted me to enter the ministry, and me not wanting
to leave my comfort zone, had become a heavy burden. In the privacy of my car early one morning, as I was making a ninety-minute
commute to a nearby city, I was having a conversation with God
about all the reasons it was just too difficult (read inconvenient) for
me to go to seminary and was proposing other ways I could serve
from where I was. But God wasn't buying my excuses. Throughout this discussion, in response to every excuse I made, God just
kept saying, "Be a pastor. Go to seminary."

I began to weep uncontrollably as I drove, crying out, "But
why me? What's so special about me? Why can't you call someone else who's more available (suggesting the names of some people
who I think would be great pastors)?" I really didn't know why I
was crying and was hoping other drivers wouldn't notice, but I
couldn't stop. Suddenly, through my tears, I heard myself saying,

"Thank you for calling me. I will go to seminary. I will trust in you and your plan for me. Show me where to go and I will." It seemed that all of the sudden, somehow, in the midst of my tears, my will was conformed to God's will for me.

A feeling of peace washed over me, which I understood to be God assuring me that all was well, that my fears were unwarranted and that he would provide for my family. I was able to pull myself together, as I arrived at my destination, and put in a full day's work.

Several days later, I was reading a devotional that explained that sometimes, in the presence of the Holy Spirit, a person weeps uncontrollably. I then understood that during that early morning commute, the weeping that I couldn't stop, or explain, occurred because I had experienced the presence of the Holy Spirit in a very real and personal way.

Roy Nelson is an attorney, mediator, and arbitrator. He will enter seminary in 2003 in preparation for the ordained ministry.

Amy Yarnall

O Lord, you have searched me and known me. You know when I sit down and when I rise up; you discern my thoughts from far away. You search out my path and my lying down and are acquainted with all of my ways.
— Psalm 139:1-3

I began my earnest search for what I should be doing with my life after graduating from college and beginning to attend Skyline UMC with my husband Ray. I had a degree in International Relations and no idea what I was supposed to be doing in terms of a vocation. My search was rooted in my intuitive, then unnamable, conviction of the truth of Psalm 139. I knew that God searches and knows me completely. I cannot put my finger on an exact moment, but I know that somewhere in 1994, I began to pray. This was the beginning of a nearly three-year time of discernment. At first, I felt foolish as I prayed. I wasn't even certain I believed in God. But still, I prayed for guidance from the God who knows me completely, about what it is that I am to do in life. The thought of ordained ministry had come to my mind as a child in confirmation classes. That thought of ordained ministry didn't recur until I was in this three-year time of discernment. Then, each time it occurred, I would shove it aside and think, "I could never do that; I just wish I could figure out what I should be doing with my life."

I changed jobs once, and continued to be miserable, longing for some insight, some guidance, into how it is that I am supposed to live this life which I have been given. I also continued my journey of faith. My questions that had begun, "How can I believe?" shifted to "How can I not believe?" God was, indeed, working within me, giving me the most precious gift I have ever, and will ever, receive: the gift of faith. Perhaps one of my greatest fears is the thought of once again facing that horrible doubt with which I wrestled. I am comforted that, if and when I come to another desert like that in my life, I will be armed with the spiritual disciplines to survive the desert, like meditating on Psalm 139, and other passages of scripture. (But it is not something to which I would look forward — not that anyone would!)

I did Bible study and served in the church and in mission outreach, and through this was opened to God's call upon my life. When I was driving home on a Friday night in January of 1997, I was in a driving trance, praying again about what God wanted me to be doing in life. I felt so weary, and I was praying, "Surely this is not what you intend for my life." Then, I had this image of my pastor serving communion at church and what I call a "God-thought" entered my mind. It was, "You need to hurry up and follow your calling while you are young." I snapped out of my trance, and wondered what exactly had just happened. I decided to sleep on it, and then discussed it with my husband and our mutual friend, Susan, who was staying with us for the weekend. They were extremely affirming of the idea of me going into ordained ministry. So, I made an appointment with my pastor and told her about my experience. She was also very affirming and encouraging. As I continued the journey, meeting with the District Committee, applying to seminary, and all of the other steps in the process that year, I still wrestled with doubt. So, my calling has a second part to it. I heard God speaking to me another time, this time through a saint of the Skyline church named Bunky Dankle. I arrived at church for a mid-week Lenten reflection and communion service and saw Bunky sitting alone. Her husband had recently died, so I went and took a seat beside her. We talked and visited for a while and then the worship service began. Throughout the service, I was distracted as I doubted and wondered whether I could really be a pastor. All I remember about the actual worship service is my pastor breaking the bread and holding up the cup. Then, at the end of the service, Bunky turned to me, took my hand into both of hers, and with tears in her eyes, she said, "Thank you for sharing your love."

Kenneth Lyerly

Five years ago, I made a decision to enter the ministry. While on a trip to North Carolina for a family reunion, I visited with my cousin, James. I shared with James that I had made a decision to go into the ministry. He looked at me in an odd way and said, "You are not going to believe what I am going to tell you." He said, "You may not remember that our grandmother Lyerly was known for having visions. When I was eight years old, I went to her and asked her if she had ever had a vision about me. She said, 'No, but I did have a vision about Kenny. In my vision, Kenny was a preacher.' " James said that this whole scene had come back to him, just that morning. I was speechless. I had remembered my grandmother having visions, but had never questioned her. She was the person in my life that read scripture to me when I was very young. She died when I was ten years old. I was 56 years old when I entered the ministry. It took 48 years for her vision to bear fruit.

Doris Miller

Up until a few years ago, I had been successfully ignoring God's call to ministry with lots of "me-rationalizing" and "why would you want me" — the typical kind of stuff. As it just so happened, a good friend was preparing for her seminary interview and visit. Since the seminary was in my home state, I offered to go along just to keep her company. The time came for her interview and visiting of classes. She gave me the car keys so that I could go to the mall if I got bored, but I decided to spend some time in the library. Things were going well at first. I flitted around the library, feeling excited by everything I saw. I had finally settled down to reading when an insistent nagging began! God began to encourage me to ministry. I was having none of it — lots of mental arguing going on. The intensity began to increase and I decided that it was time to go the mall!

When I got to the parking lot, I attempted to unlock the car for my excursion to the mall, only to find that I was unable to unlock any of the car doors! A look in the trunk told me that I wasn't going to be able to get into the car that way either. Frustrated beyond belief, I returned to the library. Time seemed not to matter, so I cannot say how long it was, but the urgency to consider ministry became greater, until finally I agreed to consider the idea. It was not long after that concession that my friend finished up and came to find me. And of course, as you might surmise, the car doors all opened with ease.

It took me several days before I could express what had happened to her, my husband, or anyone else. I did eventually agree to more than consideration of ministry! Since then, I have served nine years as a pastor, and have moved on to a new side of my call — to specialized ministry in Christian education.

How Can I Do This?

Then I said, "Ah, Lord God! Truly I do not know
how to speak, for I am only a boy." But the Lord
said to me, "Do not say, 'I am only a boy'; for you
shall go to all to whom I send you, and you shall
speak whatever I command you. Do not be afraid
of them, for I am with you to deliver you, says the
Lord." (vv. 6-8)

Kai McClinton

In 1995, at the age of 25, I was diagnosed with multiple sclerosis. I felt as if God had let me down, abandoned me. I thought that I was being punished. I fell into a depression for three years. Feeling and knowing that I wouldn't be able to walk well, or run, was very painful to me. And to top this off, God was calling me into the ministry.

"How can I do this?" I asked God over and over again. "How can I minister or visit the sick when I can hardly walk?"

God came to me with an answer that totally changed my thinking. In January of 1997, I was serving as a student pastor, and I went to a religious bookstore to buy supplies for the children at church. I gathered my items and walked to the cashier counter. A woman rang up my items, and she took my name for their mailing list. I thanked her, and as I walked away she ran after me and said, "You're not working because of your disability."

I looked at her, stunned. I had not told her that I had MS, or anything about my situation. She went on to tell me that she was blessed with a gift by which she could communicate with the spirit within another person. She said that as we were talking, her spirit was talking to my spirit, telling her of my anguish.

She said that God did not do this to me, that God was going to cure me, and that I was to continue working for the Lord. I stood there, in shock, smiling and speechless. I thanked her and told her I would continue to work for God. Then I left with tears of joy in my eyes, once again assured that God had not left me, even in my time of pain and frustration.

Six months later, I went back to that religious store and I asked the staff and the manager where this woman was. They said no woman fitting that description had ever worked there. I felt a chill go through me, because I knew I had seen an Angel of God, and I was given a promise from God. This is a promise I still believe in, for today, in January, 2003, I am walking without my cane, and I am much stronger. God is still in the healing business. Praise the Lord!

Phil Gilman

My "vision" occurred in the early morning, as I lay in bed, neither asleep nor awake. All I "heard" was a voice; I did not "see" anything. The voice said, "Your gramma prayed for you." This came at a time after I had left the church, feeling very betrayed and abandoned by God, but was tentatively taking steps back. I was unsure if I was acceptable, either to the church or to God. When I heard this voice, I knew that God accepted me, "Just As I Am," whether the church did or not.

I Saw The Lord

... I saw the Lord sitting on a throne, high and lofty;
and the hem of his robe filled the temple. (v. 1b)

Bill Penaz

In 1965, I attended a Lenten worship service at my church. Seated about three or four rows from the front of the sanctuary, I listened to people murmuring behind me and wondered why they were talking, not praying. As my eyes looked over the chancel, I found myself focusing on the cross on the altar, about fifteen feet away. The cross was about fifteen inches high and made of wood. Although I was not thinking of anything in particular, I kept my eyes focused on that cross, and suddenly it disappeared and I saw Jesus in all his glory! I saw him standing there in a white, white robe, the whitest thing I have ever seen. His beard was black and he had flowing black hair. His body was outlined in the most beautiful color of gold I have ever seen.

I was dumbstruck, but I noticed I could see only him, not the cross. I also noticed that the people in the church were still murmuring, and I thought, *Why doesn't anyone kneel? They must see what is happening!* Then I thought, *Why doesn't my wife say or do something?* I looked at her, then glanced back at the cross and Jesus was gone.

I looked at my watch, trying to figure out how much time had elapsed, and it seemed only ten seconds or so. In thinking back on it later, I did remember that I could not see the face of Jesus, but all the rest I remember so clearly.

I have only told about five people very close to me about this. They looked at me as if I was kind of strange! I don't mind. I only wish I could describe it more precisely, because it was the most beautiful thing that I have ever seen!

While praying, I found myself on the suspension footbridge over the Pike River in the Fiordland National Park, an area where I worked as a guide one summer. As I was crossing, a huge rainbow trout leapt up from the river and fastened its jaws onto the edge of the bridge: an impossible leap for a trout, I might add. There it hung, and I knew that all I had to do was slip my finger into its gills and it was mine: the biggest trout I would ever catch. But would I have caught it?

Even in my visionary state I was anxious. I had no fishing rod, no flies, and no license! How could I possibly claim this fish? It would be against the law. Then the fish smiled at me: a huge, laughing, fishy smile! I bent down quickly and scooped it up. I had known grace as a doctrine for a long time, but that day it became a living part of me.

The Gift Of Trees

Pamela J. Tinnin

Blessed are those who trust in the Lord, whose trust is in the Lord. They shall be like a tree planted by water, sending out its roots by the stream. (vv. 7-8a)

I remember the first time I planted trees. It was almost thirty years ago, on a dairy farm on the side of a mountain in Oregon. The farm belonged to two brothers in their eighties, shy bachelors who lived in the house they had built in the latter 1920s. The Steinhaurs had emigrated from Germany and had hoped to marry and raise families in America. Somehow marriage had never happened for either of them, so they grew old together, the big house echoing with the clomp of their boots in the kitchen, and the sound of their voices at breakfast each morning, planning the day's chores.

We met by accident. Friends of mine lived down the road from them and fairly frequently I'd drive past their place, always admiring how well-kept it was — fences and buildings painted white, a fine-looking barn with an arched roof, and their fruit tree orchard with neatly-pruned apple, pear, and cherry trees.

One day I saw one of their Brown Swiss cows wandering on the road. Off to the right, there was an open gate. I stopped the car and cautiously approached. The cow was placid enough, and ambled towards the gate, plodding along, tail switching back and forth. Just as she walked into the pasture, the brothers drove up in an old Ford pickup. They couldn't thank me enough and insisted I come up to the house for a cup of tea.

After we introduced ourselves, they bustled around the kitchen. Harald set out cups and saucers, three worn silver spoons, a jar of amber honey, a small pitcher of thick cream, and a plate of Oreo cookies. Oscar filled the teapot and put it on the stove, then cut a lemon into thin slices. I noticed when they sat down, they bowed their heads for just a moment, whispered a prayer, and crossed themselves.

They asked me all kinds of questions — about my parents, my husband and children, where I was from, why I had moved to Scotts Mills. In turn, they told me of growing up in Germany, of the war years, of the terrible times after the war. In 1921, their parents, wanting something better for their sons, scraped together everything they had and sent them to the United States, knowing they would probably never see them again.

I never did get to my friends' house that day. The brothers wanted to show me their orchard, and we spent the afternoon in the warm spring sunshine, the air sweet with the smell of apple blossoms and loud with the buzzing that came from the white box beehives at the far end of the field.

Over the next year, I spent a lot of time with Harald and Oscar. Not only did I enjoy their company, but I yearned to be a farmer and I knew they were the kind of farmers I dreamed of being. One of the times I remember most was when we planted trees. By then they were 83 and 85, but still able to put in a hard day's work. We planted a half dozen trees that afternoon, two apples and two pears in the orchard, and two elm trees up near the house, small spindly sticks without a sign of life. It was one of those days that stay in your memory as being as close to perfect as a day can be.

Not a month after that, Oscar died quietly in his sleep. Afterwards, Harald went rapidly downhill. Within a year, the Social Services people stepped in, auctioned off the cows, equipment, and belongings, and moved Harald to Salem to live in a nursing home. I dreamed of buying the farm, of keeping it just like they did, but I had no money. It sold for over a third above market value to city people looking for a weekend retreat.

In the next months, I visited Harald often. Even after he stopped speaking, he still smiled with pleasure when he saw me. It wasn't long, though, before my family and I moved away. For several years I wrote letters, sent Christmas and birthday cards, but I never heard from him again, not until the day one of my cards was returned stamped "addressee deceased."

When I think of the afternoon we planted the trees, I can almost hear the sound of Harald's voice, the heavy German accent that seemed to become more pronounced the longer I knew him. "You may ask why we plant trees," he said, "two old men, with no children, no family. Well, Miss Pamela, we plant trees for God."

They were my friends; two old men who some people might have thought had little to show for their lives, just a small mountain farm that in the end was sold to strangers. Years after they'd gone, I drove up that winding road to see their place one last time. I knew it would be different and it was. The house was painted green, a deck added to the front, and a swimming pool behind. But the barn looked the same, and beyond it, the orchard still stood. When I saw it, it took my breath away, a field of white and pink blossoms so thick I couldn't see the branches on the trees.

I thought of Harald and Oscar, who, with generous and loving hearts, poured their lives into one small portion of creation. For over sixty years, they not only gave of their time and money to their church, they tended the land with respect and care, treated their animals with kindness, and were always quick to help their neighbors. When I met them, they were near the end of their journey, but they were still opening their home to strangers and planting trees for God. If we answer God's call, can we do any less?

God Stories

Judy Snyder Stout

> *So it is with the resurrection of the dead. What is*
> *sown is perishable, what is raised is imperishable.*
> *It is sown in weakness, it is raised in power. It is*
> *sown a physical body, it is raised a spiritual body.*
> *If there is a physical body, there is also a spiritual*
> *body.* (vv. 42-44)

My father was my life, and in 1989 he and Mom came to live with me, literally to die. We had him until May 31, 1991, when I walked into his room and he looked at me and died. I felt my world go with him. I wanted to lie down beside him and go with him. But, I was only 53 with five grown children and a husband.

The next six months were filled with such unspeakable grief and depression that, at times, I couldn't put one foot in front of another.

The "God stories" started the day after my father died: my mother was in a nursing home with Alzheimer's, and when we walked into the room, she actually put a complete sentence together and asked if we were going to leave her like "her man" did. For the fifteen weeks that she lived after that, she kept telling us "her man" was outside the window or down at the end of the hall. The nurses kept turning her around, but she still saw her man. I would take walks with her to let her see her man.

Then, one day, she told me that her man was leaving. Within a week, she was gone, too. I mentioned that my father was my life. My mother was not. But from the day they walked into the house, my life was filled with "God stories"!

About six months later, I woke from a dream to such a blinding light that I could not open my eyes. But I "saw" my father standing at the foot of some steps, with his arm around my mother, who was standing on his right-hand side. She did not say a word, but it was such a shock to see her standing, since she had just lost her right leg before she died.

He told me not to worry anymore, that he felt wonderful (he had been in horrible pain due to cancer), and not to grieve. He told me that he loved me and to take care. Then he was gone.

The next day, I called my daughters to tell them about my "dream." My oldest daughter replied, "Mom! You won't believe it! I woke up in the middle of the night, and Grandpa was at the foot of the bed! He told me he loves me and not to miss him!"

My youngest daughter, when I told her about the "dream," said, "He came to me, too." That started our journey into so many "God stories" that I ended up in ministry, and now serve as a part-time local pastor in the United Methodist church. I wouldn't trade it for the world!

A Vision Of Light

Mary Downing

And while he was praying, the appearance of his face changed, and his clothes became dazzling white. Suddenly they saw two men, Moses and Elijah, talking to him. They appeared in glory and were speaking of his departure, which he was about to accomplish at Jerusalem. (vv. 29-31)

It was a summer evening in the year 2000 when four of us, friends through church for more than twenty years, decided spur-of-the-moment to drive from Port Washington to Hartford, Wisconsin, to make what we knew in our hearts would be a final visit with our dear friend, Valerie Arveson. For several years, Val had been waging a courageous struggle against ovarian cancer. The end was imminent. We needed to say good-bye.

We arrived, hesitantly, at Val's home. How do we do this? What can be said? How terribly kind it was of her even to allow us to come.

As we entered her living room, Val's husband, Arv, was completing tubal administration of the liquids that had been sustaining her for some time. We sat down and it was immediately apparent that this was the first time we had ever been with Val that she didn't have the energy to be Val anymore. Her role tonight would be as listener.

We hadn't been there long when one in our group, Jean, got up, walked across the living room, and sat down next to Val on the sofa. Taking Val's hands in her own, and sitting almost face to face, Jean proceeded to share her story. Amidst gulping sobs, and to the total amazement of the rest of us, she poured out a story of light and peace, comfort and incredible love.

You see Jean, too, was undergoing treatment for cancer at that time. While her health had not yet declined to the end stage, as Val's had, I strongly believe that, in her heart, she knew victory would not be experienced here on earth. What Jean had experienced, and needed so urgently to share with Val, had happened to her within the last several months.

Early one morning, Jean was awakened by a startling and intense light — brighter and warmer than anything she had ever seen or felt before. It filled the room. Then a voice, that she was certain belonged to God, said to her, "It's not time to go yet." The experience lasted only briefly, but over and over again, Jean said to Val, "You have nothing to fear. The love that enveloped me at that moment was greater than anything I have ever felt in my life. I didn't want it to end. I was transported to a place so beautiful, so wonderful, that it defies description. Nothing in my worldly experience could even begin to compare."

Following this pre-dawn experience, Jean's initial reaction was to remain silent. Who could possibly understand? Folks would consider her crazy. It was too personal and too life-changing to share. Being seated in Val's home, however, surrounded by long-time friends in faith, changed that. Seeing a dear friend so close to death loosened the bonds, and it was as though Jean was propelled across the living room. Remaining silent was no longer an option. News of the glory that awaited Val in the next life had to be shared.

Reactions to Jean's story varied among the rest of us. It was so amazing and we were so unprepared. Some of us felt a little bit cheated. Each of us came intending to say good-bye. Opportunity for that diminished as the evening became totally centered around this one amazing experience.

Jean's admission of being not only ready, but also anxious to die, left us confused. We wanted her to continue fighting and she was saying no, the future held such incomparable glory, it was to be embraced, anticipated, longed for. Her words to Val were, "You go and I will follow."

A month or so later, on September 26, 2000, Valerie died. Cancer took Jean's life on November 10, 2001. Each of these women, in her own personal and private way, approached death fearlessly. The fight had been long and painful. They were ready to share the Light.

Lent

Having seen and experienced what cannot be expressed in words and still must be communicated, the astronauts and cosmonauts gave words to my own experience of priesthood. It is a grace, it allows me to see a vision, and it is a call to let others know what I have seen....

Henry Nouwen

.

Henry J. M. Nouwen, *Sabbatical Journey* (New York: The Crossroads Publishing, 1998), p. 23.

Abounding In Steadfast Love

Yet even now, says the Lord, return to me with all
your heart, with fasting and with weeping, and with
mourning; rend your hearts and not your cloth-
ing. Return to the Lord, your God, for he is gra-
cious and merciful, slow to anger, and abounding
in steadfast love, and relents from punishing. (vv.
12-13)

Ralph Milton

Our son, Lloyd, died on May 4, 1997. His death was a terrible
shock to all of us, but most particularly to his twin sister Grace.
But as we gathered a small group of family around us in a little
memorial service to say good-bye to Lloyd, Grace told the story of
a remarkable dream she'd had — a dream that ministered to all of
us.

To appreciate the meaning of the dream, you need to know that
Lloyd had never known how to give or receive affection. The fetal
alcohol syndrome he suffered at birth and the abuse of his first two
years in a foster home made it impossible for him to know that he
was loved, or that he had been endowed with many gifts.

In the dream, Lloyd had been sitting with Grace on the edge of
her bed, and giving her a big hug. "Then he said, 'I have found our
father.' At first I thought he meant our birth father, but then I realized he meant God."

At the end of our memorial service, we heard a tape of a pia-
nist playing "The Rose." Lloyd had a gift of music, but could not
believe the gift, and so didn't develop it. But he loved that song,
perhaps because it spoke of the potential so many of us saw in him,
of the "seed" that, it seems, needed to die beneath the snows so that

somehow, somewhere, it can blossom "with the sun's love" into a rose.

We ache with the loss of our son, and wish he could have changed his last and final choice. But it was his. And we know that Lloyd had learned how to love, and that he has found God. The rose has blossomed. We are in pain, but we are at peace.

Ralph Milton, *Angels In Red Suspenders: An Unconventional and Humorous Approach to Spirituality* (Ontario: Northstone Publishing, Inc., 1997), pp. 282-283. Reprinted with permission.

Rebecca Coan-Henderleiter

On December 19, 2001, I felt as if my life was spinning out of control. The reasons for what I did are not as important as the results. So I'll skip the details and get to the point — I made the decision to end my life.

After stopping at a pharmacy and picking up an assortment of over-the-counter medications that I knew would poison and then quickly kill me, I drove to a remote area of a local forest preserve and took all of the pills. I took something to make me fall asleep and eventually stop my breathing, something else to prevent me from vomiting in case I started seizing, and another bottle of pills to cause irreversible liver and kidney damage just in case someone found me unconscious. About fifteen minutes after I began falling asleep, my ex-husband called me on my cell phone. He could tell something was wrong and I confessed that I was in the process of dying, but refused to tell him where I was. He called my best friend and the police. I don't remember much, except having all of them on the phone at the same time — the police and both of them — while they frantically tried to figure out what I had taken and where I was. Something I said must have given them a clue, because one of the last things I remember before passing out was a sheriff reaching in my truck and pulling me out. It had been almost an hour since I had taken the pills.

I was put in an ambulance. The paramedics kept telling me to stay awake as they forced liquid charcoal down my throat. Then I felt my body fall backwards and my soul slip out of my body through my feet. Suddenly I was engulfed in a bright, white light and I felt a loving Presence with me. The Presence was angry, not in a harsh, vindictive way, but more like a loving parent disappointed in a child.

"Do you realize what you have done?" asked the Presence.

"I'm sorry," I said. "I couldn't handle my life anymore. It was a living hell."

"That was not Hell. That was your path and I was with you all along. You cannot choose which lessons you need to learn. You lost your faith and turned your back on me. It is not your time to be with me, so you must go elsewhere."

The Presence and light were gone. I was in complete darkness and felt utterly alone. It was extremely uncomfortable. The place I was in was too hot, but at the same time too cold. A horrible odor permeated the place. It was completely offensive, unlike anything I had ever smelled before. A piercing noise filled my ears. My eyes began seeing death all around me. Dead trees, dried bones, a vast gray horizon of nothingness, no color. There were others there, but they were totally unaware of each other's presence. Some walked in circles, bumping into others without realizing they were there. Others just screamed and wailed. Everyone was lost.

"Gi Manado (Great Spirit)," I screamed, "save me! Jesus, please forgive my sins!"

Immediately I was pulled back into the Light.

"My child, your faith and repentance have saved you from damnation. Now you must go back and finish your path."

"No," I cried, "I can't go back to that living hell you put me in. It was too much for me. I'm not strong enough. Surely there are others who can do your will."

"You were created for a purpose and that is your life's work. Your life's work is unfinished. You must go somewhere to fulfill a destiny."

Suddenly I found myself terrified and running for my life. I was sweating and exhausted, but I kept up with the herd. Shots were being fired from everywhere. Then a soldier on horseback got next to me and shot me in the spine. I went down. The pain was excruciating. I tried to get up but could only move my front legs. Only then did I realize I was a buffalo somewhere in the 1800s. My human spirit was in the body of a dying buffalo. I still felt human emotions and was totally aware that the Presence had sent me here. But why?

I wanted to live, to survive, but my hind legs failed me. I was completely exhausted and losing blood very rapidly. As I looked up at the hot sun, I could see the vultures circling closer and closer. They began landing around me and started tearing at my open wound. My cries for help came out in the sound of a dying animal.

"God, save me!" I screamed in my buffalo grunt. Still the torturous death continued.

"Lord, why have you forsaken me?" I cried. "Jesus, help me! Guidu (Mother Earth), Gi Manado, help me! Wonkatonka (God) Creator, Great Spirit, Raphael, Gabriel, Michael, Saint Francis, Mother Mary, Allah, Buddha, whoever you are please stop this! Yahweh, where are you?"

At that moment, I felt my spirit lifted up. I looked down over the field where hundreds of buffalo lay dying. And then I was pulled, again, into the Presence of the white light.

"Who are you?" I asked. "I called out the name of so many gods and angels and saints. Who answered?"

"I did. I am all. I am the One God, the Creator. Many may see me in different ways, but all those who look for good and righteousness find me in one form or another. For you, I am the God of your childhood and the God of your ancestors. I gave you a new life, as you requested. That life was a living hell, much unlike your true life, which you describe as such. Your journey has been difficult, but for all of it there was a purpose — for you to do great works. You were born a healer and a warrior. Some of your life lessons have given you the gifts you need in order to heal others and fight against injustices."

"I don't believe anything positive has come from my life," I replied. "It just seems like there was always so much pain. I haven't made much of a difference in the world."

"Look at your life, without the pain. See all that has happened and what became of it."

I watched as the Creator showed me different phases of my life. I saw the worst — molestation as a child, rapes as a teenager, drug addiction, mental illness, abusive relationships, leaving my husband. Then every bad experience shone as it showed its connection to good. It was the incredible amount of strength I was given to live through those ordeals, which gave me the ability to empathize with others who had similar experiences. I saw my unwavering strength to stand up against injustice towards others, one person at a time. My faith gave faith to others, who passed it on. There was a huge chain reaction every time I passed hope on to another. And even in the worst of times, my God was there, giving me the strength to survive and persevere. My life suddenly made sense.

"Your journey is not complete. You must return to your path."

"I want to stay with you."

"Now is not the time. You will return in my time, not yours. If you choose to follow my will, you will find that there is much more in life that awaits you. If you choose to turn your back on my will, you will be without the Light of Life forever, or you may choose to take the place of more dying buffalo spirits. You will be with me, because I have always been with you."

"Please forgive me, Father. I will go back and do your work. I believe you will remain with me. I beg you to let me go back if it's not too late. My body has been so badly poisoned, I'm afraid to return to it."

"All will be well and you will be healed."

A bright purple flash surrounded me. Suddenly, I felt someone pushing on my chest. I gasped for air.

"She's back," someone yelled.

"How long was she down?"

"Two minutes."

"Rebecca! Open your eyes."

I was back in the ambulance.

I spent five days in an intensive care unit, where I was treated for the overdose while doctors monitored my liver and kidneys.

81

My doctor was amazed that I showed no signs of any internal damage whatsoever. Then I was transferred to a psychiatric ward for another four days.

My psychiatrist said it best. "You didn't *attempt* suicide; you *committed* suicide. There is no medical reason why you're sitting here talking to me. With what you did to your body, the very best we could have hoped for was you being in a coma, dying of liver failure. God gave you a second chance, and I hope to see you make the most of it. But if you walk into my office as a buffalo, there's not much I can do for you."

Leslie Powell Sadasivan

I have been blessed with mystical experiences since my fourteen-year-old gay son's death. Robbie committed suicide after years of homophobic teasing and harassment at school. He could not find peace with his sexuality because of the effects of this harassment and his struggle with God and the church's anti-gay doctrine. He could not see a future.

Robbie was a very spiritual child. He asked me a week before his suicide if I was sure there was a heaven. He also wrote on his high school book covers, "God made me this way." After his death I found poetry that describes his pain.

Before Robbie's suicide, I was stressed by trying to help him adjust to the pain and isolation of being gay. Despite our restrictions, he kept going on the Internet to talk to other gays and view gay pornography. I kept praying to God to help Robbie and to help our family help him. Two weeks before Robbie died, my husband Peter had been working in his study, and I had gone to bed early. Something wakened me from a sound sleep. I looked around the bedroom, thinking Peter had come to bed, but what I saw was an opaque, circular light hovering over Peter's side of the bed. I went to tell Peter what I had seen right away, because I wanted to assure myself that I wasn't dreaming. I thought it was a sign from God that everything would be okay for Robbie, who had been started on a new antidepressant the week before. Later, I realized that it was a sign from God, telling me that God was with me during this most painful time of my life.

After Robbie's suicide, I learned about the homophobic teasing and harassment he had endured. I kept praying to God to show me how to help keep others from suffering the way Robbie did. I felt inspired by God and Robbie to tell his story, so I contacted several local newspapers and eventually it was printed in four Cleveland newspapers and the *Ladies Home Journal.* Our largest paper, *The Plain Dealer*, placed his story on the Sunday paper's front page. It helped to inspire many to activism toward making schools safe for youth perceived to be gay, who are teased and harassed by their peers. Our Gay Center created a Safe Schools Are For Everyone program, for which I am a speaker. With the aid of much prayer, I have shared Robbie's story through speeches to teachers, students, and counselors. It is only through God's grace that I am able to do this, because I am very uncomfortable as a public speaker.

I have had other spiritual signs from Robbie that have helped me to deal with his death. A year after his burial, I awoke at 2:00 a.m. to find the halogen lamp in our bedroom turned on. I woke my husband, but he knew nothing about it. He had not turned it on, as we rarely use the lamp. I felt that it had been Robbie, and went into his bedroom to pray and talk to him. I felt his presence and wept joyfully. The lamp has never turned on that way again. I have had three dreams about Robbie. In the dreams he is always coming back for a visit, looking very peaceful and happy. They are so very real that when I wake it seems like he was really with me. It is a great comfort. And there have been other, smaller signs.

Living without Robbie is the hardest thing I have ever had to do. Giving the speeches takes an incredible amount of courage. I know it is God who continues to help me. I never seek speaking engagements — they come to me. I think and pray about them, and I do say no to some, but most of them I agree to, especially those for teachers and schools. It is only with God's grace that I have the courage to go on.

83

Angel, You Are

Kerri Sherwood

For he will command his angels concerning you
to guard you in all your ways. (v. 11)

It's not that I ever feel that my brother is far away. It's just that, so often, I would love to sit over coffee with him or watch him work on my 1971 bug car. I think he must feel the same way.

I am the youngest of three, separated by nine and eleven years from my older brother and sister, respectively. They included me in their lives as they lived at home and then moved on to establishing their own homes. Some of my memories with them are more vivid than others, and I can distinctly see, in my mind's eye, a picture of my brother taking me, many times, for a ride on the back of his bike.

As I sat at his hospital bedside, with the intrusion of a chemical drip in his arm battling the lung cancer that had invaded his body, we played an inane game of Battleship and said huge things to each other that will echo in my brain always ... as he told me how proud he was of me ... his little sister.

When Wayne died, I felt an incredible loss — this person I had idolized my whole life was no longer here to hang out with. But I became aware of his presence, through little and big moments since then, keeping me safe or meeting people he would seemingly want to be a part of my life.

I believe he is just on the other side and can make himself known to me at whim.

I pulled into the Ohio Turnpike service area to fill the van's gas tank on one of my many fifteen-hour road trips touring as a musician. Parking next to the gas pump, I got out to fill the car with gas when I saw on the all-white pump, in raised white letters, the word "Wayne." I drove away from a gig in Cincinnati and happened to glance to the right of the interstate to see a big building with the word "Wayne" written across it. The traffic was congested, so I was concentrating on my driving outside of the Seattle airport, when I felt a sudden need to look at the sign on the side of the road. It read "Wayne." The day I finished recording some tracks for a new project, I started to drive home from Nashville. I felt sad. Very sad. It was the anniversary of Wayne's death. As I drove, I found myself looking for a sign of him; I had come to expect them. I had already traveled about six hours when I impatiently said aloud, "Where are you, Bro? I need you today!" It wasn't but a few minutes later when a truck passed by on my right and I felt compelled to look at it. As it passed, I could see emblazoned across the side the words, "Wayne, Wayne, Wayne." Okay! I get it!

Yes, angel, you are my big brother.
I'm still riding on the back of your bike.
Always.
Thanks for the ride.

"angel you are"

when I was a little girl you always took me along with you and I
never imagined there would come a day when you couldn't go
as you rode your bike through the streets back home
you rode me along
and you took such care as you rode me there
my big brother so strong

now you're an angel in my life
and i'm still ridin' on the back of your bike
you've got the handlebars firm in your hand
leadin' me through unfamiliar land
you're my big brother till the end of all time
angel you are
angel you are

85

now i'm all grown up and in charge of just where I go yet I
always seem to see reminders of you everywhere, I know
that you're there, you are always there,
you're still leadin' the way
somehow you still take care as I go here and there
even from far away

'cause you're an angel in my life
and i'm still ridin' on the back of your bike
you've got the handlebars firm in your hand
leadin' me through unfamiliar land
you're my big brother till the end of all time
angel you are
angel you are

now it seems to me that you can still somehow be a part
when you choose to be you can be here, you're not just part of my
    heart ...

'cause you're an angel in my life
and i'm still ridin' on the back of your bike
you've got the handlebars firm in your hand
leadin' me through unfamiliar land
you're my big brother till the end of all time
angel you are
angel you are

(copyright 2002 kerri sherwood from the album *as sure as the sun*)

The song "angel you are" is included on the Kerri Sherwood album *as sure as the sun*. This album can be purchased through the
recording label Sisu Music Productions, Inc. toll-free 800-651-SISU
(7478), through the website www.kerrisherwood.com, through
Amazon.com or retail stores nationwide. Kerri has seven other albums currently released.

Deliverance

For he will hide me in his shelter in the day of trouble; he will conceal me under the cover of his tent; he will set me high on a rock. (v. 5)

Laura Hoff

There was a time when my husband and I were very poor. We had three young children and a home to pay for, car payments ... and I was trying to stay at home with our children and did not contribute to our income at all. All around us it seemed that everyone had more than we had. Our cars were junky and I shopped at St. Vincent's for our clothes. I was constantly, though maybe not consciously, comparing my life with my friends' and feeling frustrated and even angry with them for having more than I had.

At one particularly bad time, it seemed we were even about to lose our house, and I had to ask my parents for food money. I didn't think I was a money waster. I had always been proud of the way I saved my family money by shopping at secondhand stores, garage sales, and estate sales. I had gone to a secondhand store that day and had bought a very cheap basket to hang on our wall. We hadn't lived in our house for very long, and we were still trying to decorate and make it a "home." I knew I shouldn't have spent even the dollar it took to buy the basket, as we had just asked my parents for money. I felt so guilty and upset by our situation. Even worse, I came home and hung the basket up and I liked it ... but it needed something. I needed some dried weeds ... possibly some German statice to put in it. I got even angrier. "See," I thought to myself, "you are never happy ... want, want, want!" My husband came home and we ended up having a fight about it. He could not understand my need for that basket at all and was angry that I spent the money. It was such a stupid little thing ... but so big.

I prayed to God fiercely that night. I didn't feel God was near. I was scared about all we could lose and about all I felt we didn't, and might never, have. I prayed, if we could never have more money, then could God please take away my desires for material things and help me to be happy and feel blessed with whatever I had instead of always wanting more. I also prayed that something would happen to help us financially, as well as something happening in my heart. I prayed this with many tears. I had had it! I was very run down with worrying about money all the time.

That night was our monthly meeting of Mothers of Preschoolers at a local church. I had been attending for years and I always enjoyed the meetings, but this evening I didn't feel like going. I was not in the mood to socialize and be receptive to anything, but I dragged myself there anyway. I pulled into the parking lot and noticed that every car but mine was a mini-van. "Look at all of these yuppies! See, everyone but us has money for a mini-van and here I pull up in my ratty car." I had three children and I could really use a mini-van! I walked into the church and found out that the topic of the evening was "Living within your means." My eyebrows went up. I wondered if God was involved in this conspiracy. The longer that meeting went on, the angrier I got! We talked in small groups about how we saved money. The other ladies talked about how they had forfeited their trip to Cancun this year! I got angrier ... and about how they kept Christmas spending to (a ridiculous amount of money) ... I got angrier. When it came time for me to speak, the tears just came down, and I shared that I honestly didn't have money for food that week. They all just looked at me like I was such a poor, pitiful thing. I was so sorry I had come and shared. I felt so out of place. I wanted to leave, but the meeting was almost over anyway, and I would have had to walk past too many with tears in my eyes. A lady stood up tentatively and said, "I have no idea why I did this, but before coming here tonight, I went out into my garden and brought a whole table full of German statice. Maybe no one is interested, but if you are, please take all you would like." Talk about tears coming down!

I drove home and carefully placed my weeds from God in my basket. Wow! He does listen to me. God gives me weeds!

Shortly thereafter, my husband got a raise and I started a job in ministry working with youth. God knows my *every* need, and even my every desire. I do not need to worry.

David Eaton

I grew up on a farm in southern Minnesota. In 1962, my father and uncle shared several farm implements, so we would help each other out. On an October Saturday, I was helping my Dad pick corn on Uncle Jerry's farm. The day was getting late, but Dad wanted to finish so he could take the equipment back to our farm to get started picking corn on Monday. (We never did farm work on Sunday, for that was the Lord's Day and a day of rest.) By the time we finished picking corn, it was dusk and our farm was over two miles away. Neither tractor had lights so we were in a hurry to get home. With instructions to follow Dad, I drove a tractor and wagon. I was probably 1,500 feet behind his equipment (tractor, corn picker, and wagon). It was getting very dark, but we were nearing the home place.

As I came around a corner, going full throttle (18 mph) on the John Deere B, (nine-year-olds love going full throttle), I met a vehicle coming from the other direction. Its headlights were on high beam and it had stopped on its side of the road in front of me. The light blinded me and suddenly, right in front of me, was the back of the wagon connected to the tractor my dad was driving, stopped on his side (and mine) of the road! My older brother had come looking for us and had stopped to talk with Dad. Dad didn't realize I could not see his stopped equipment.

I had just enough time to make one hard attempt to disengage the hand clutch — but it wouldn't disengage. I was standing behind the steering wheel — much like a ship's captain — when I felt the tractor being steered through my arms. My tractor and wagon entered the ditch, missing the stationary wagon by a foot, drove parallel to the wagon, corn picker, and tractor, and came up out of the ditch, missing the front of my dad's tractor by a foot! After returning to the roadway, I once again attempted to disengage the hand clutch, and this time it released easily. My dad came running and, with frantic tears in his voice, cried out, "Are you all right?" Can you imagine what had gone through his mind and heart through all of this? Calmly, I assured him that I was fine, but had lost my cap in the process.

Upon further review, some very interesting facts turned up. It was understandable to just miss the back of the stationary wagon when I entered the ditch, because I had reacted as immediately as I could. But why did I miss the front of the tractor by only a foot when coming out of the ditch? That question wasn't answered until the next morning when my dad went back to look over the scene in the daylight. Had I stayed in the ditch one second longer, I would have hit a field road culvert, connecting a farmer's field with the road, and certainly would have flipped the tractor over. He also discovered a barbed-wired fence on the field side of the ditch that could have caused me injury or worse if my tractor had veered too far to the right. And, it would have taken a professional stunt driver to have entered and left the steep ditch at just the right angle to avoid tipping over.

Anyone investigating this scene would have been foolish to suggest that it was skill, or even luck, for a nine-year-old boy to have maneuvered a tractor at full throttle through all of this while standing up! I knew that, through the power of God, Someone else had driven that tractor into and then out of that ditch, though through my hands and arms.

My mother was the first to interpret that God had a special plan and purpose for my life. He had preserved me in a special way and I had profoundly experienced his presence. Maybe that was the day, way back forty years ago, that I first began moving away from being a farmer and toward becoming a minister....

Sound Grace

Lucinda Alwa

*My soul is satisfied as with a rich feast, and my
mouth praises you with joyful lips when I think of
you on my bed, and meditate on you in the watches
of the night; for you have been my help, and in the
shadow of your wings I sing for joy.* (vv. 5-7)

Twenty-four years ago, my younger sister Charlotte died. A
few months after her death, I found myself lying awake in the middle
of the night, unable to relax. My heart felt wide open — gaping
after something. In the dark and quiet room there suddenly started
a crackling noise, like fire. It grew very loud. I looked around, but
the room was still the same. No glint of fire. I knew I was awake
because I could feel the bed sheets, blink my eyes, and pinch myself. The crackling sound that I could hear so clearly was not in the
room in the physical sense. Nothing was burning; no "thing" was
crackling. And yet my physical ears could hear the crackling as
though flames were surrounding the bed, as though I were in the
middle of raging fire.

I began to realize that this was a spiritual sound, or that I was
hearing something non-physical. I was filled with joy, disbelief,
and absolute wonder. I lay reveling in the waves of crackling, not
knowing what it was, but feeling that I was connected both with
God and with Charlotte. The crackling continued for some minutes and then slowly faded and came to a stop. I felt let down, but
I sensed that, for a brief time, I had been in God's holy space with
Charlotte.

This experience has been my treasure. I believe that God,
through the crackling, reached out and embraced me in that time
of grief. I also believe that Charlotte touched me, however strangely.
I've wondered about the significance of the crackling — was it

fire? Purifying flame? Whatever logical interpretation there may be, most precious to me is the wonder I felt in the midst of that inexplicable ocean of sound.

The loud "crackling" has never recurred. There is, however, an inner sound that I hear in quiet, when I listen with heart and spirit. This sound is at the core of my prayer life, for it brings me into Christ's presence. Though it does not come loud, like crackling fire, it is always there when I listen for it. It is the sound of peace and healing. It is the sound of God's love. And it is here.

A New Creation

So if anyone is in Christ, there is a new creation;
everything old has passed away; see, everything
has become new! (v. 17)

Debi Lyerly Lawson

I cannot remember a time when God wasn't the source of all that I am. I can recall the day I made my "official" commitment to the relationship my soul craved to have with the Almighty. It was an awesome April evening in 1983, in Orlando, Florida, at a Billy Graham Crusade. I remember leaving my seat to go up to the giant stage with hundreds of others, all of us with one collective thought: to give our lives over to Christ. I also remember feeling God in everyone and everything in that stadium. When we have such wonderful spiritual epiphanies, we don't ever want to lose those moments.

Well, as I grew older, my relationship with the Father was a contented one. I had successes and failures like every other Christian. That was where my problem was. I felt like "every other Christian." The proverbial Fourth of July fireworks were not going off in my godly world. Where were my miracles? Where was that sense of being able to conquer the whole universe just because I was a child of God? I truly felt like God was too busy to hear my prayers, let alone feel my need for some spectacular event to bring me closer to him.

I sat on my bed one evening, feeling somewhat despondent and even a little abandoned, while flipping through television channels. Nothing was ever going to pull me out of this blue funk I was in. "God, where are you?" I thought. As I jumped from one channel to the next, I got my answer: there, on one of the Christian channels, was a Billy Graham Crusade. But not just any Billy Graham crusade — it was the one being held at the Tangerine Bowl in 1983, in Orlando, Florida. And there, among all of the hundreds of people going to the stage to give up their earthly lives for more promising, fulfilling spiritual ones, was a brown-haired girl named Debi Lyerly.

God did hear my prayers and he felt my needs deeper than I ever could have. He had brought me back to the place I had forgotten years ago. And at that moment, I could feel God in everything. As I watched myself being saved some twenty years ago, I realized that our most important accomplishments and greatest joys are also God's most important accomplishments and greatest joys. He, too, feels our happiness. And just as we struggle through our doubts and heartaches, our Heavenly Father suffers as well. I know now, as I have always truly known, that God never leaves us. He would never desert us. But, mostly, he never ever stops listening to us or loving us.

Jim Schlosser

It was back in 1986, as I recall, that I felt the power of God as I was enshrouded in what seemed to be glory all around me. A Catholic priest, whom I considered to be a good friend, had given me an audio tape to listen to.

The tape contained the personal testimony of Father John Bertolucci, the man who was apparently instrumental in starting the charismatic movement within the Roman Catholic Church. Naturally, I was very curious, having been a practicing Catholic myself for over 47 years before finding the truth about Christ through a home Bible study. I had been born again and was hungry for God's word. I was also glad to hear that this charismatic movement was gaining great ground within the fertile hearts of so many Catholics.

As I listened to his testimony, I began to feel a powerful presence within myself. On the tape, he was relating his experience at a home Bible study where another priest laid his hands on Father

Bertolucci's head and prayed for him. At that point he was overcome by what he believed was the power of God, and he felt a spiritual cleansing which he had never before in his life received.

It was at exactly that same point in the tape when I felt the same thing. I was mesmerized! I felt unable to move, and I felt so peaceful as I fell to my knees and sobbed and laughed. All that I was able to utter was, "Jesus, I love you." Over and over again I continued to sob, laugh, and praise my savior, the result being that I felt so spiritually cleansed and at peace with God myself that it took me most of that night to settle back and realize what had happened.

From that day on, I have had a continuing love for God's word and certainly an ever-increasing love for Jesus.

Joy L. Kilby

In the early 1970s, soon after the birth of our son, my husband and I began to argue over even the smallest things. Ours was not the happy-ever-after marriage I had read about in fairy tales. My heart felt empty and full of longing. We tried marriage counseling with the pastor of our church, and he said one thing that made a lot of sense to me: With God, nothing is impossible. I understood that Jesus and the written word bring truth and life to those who seek, and I began seeking. However, my husband and I were divorced not long after that, and my son and I left the church.

Now I was divorced, a single mother, and churchless! I felt totally confused, but not yet broken. Not long after my divorce, I began to date a man I met in a bar. A year later, we got married. My son was now seven years old. I desperately wanted a father figure for him, since his own father had moved to Texas and had little contact with him.

I started a new life with a new husband. His mother was even religious, and I counted that as a positive. We could talk scripture, and I was happy with that, but as time went on, I felt that something was going wrong. I hadn't known that he was an alcoholic, although we met in a bar and I should have taken the clues. I didn't know how sick he was and how under bondage to alcohol. We were married for a total of sixteen years. Drinking made him sarcastic, and he began to abuse both my son and me verbally. We had two sons together, and he gave all of his attention to them, just to hurt me, telling them that I was sick and that they didn't have to listen to me.

Five years into the marriage, I began to cry out to God, "I don't understand. Please help me!" I didn't understand my life or its direction. Later that year, I went to a rummage sale. When Grandma was alive, she used to say, "It would be Heaven to die at a rummage." Well, as I was standing, looking at some books, I heard a voice behind me. It was a man's voice, gentle and authoritative. I turned around, but there was no one there. The voice seemed to come from within me, yet behind me, and then I realized that it was a spirit talking to me. He said, "You are being deceived." I could hardly stand up. My knees became weak. I gripped the table to keep from falling.

"Oh, my Lord!" I answered. "I've never really known you as Lord!" I was beginning to understand. The darkness was beginning to fade. The Day Star had risen in my heart. I personally committed myself into the Lord's hands, to teach me, step by step. Jesus, Lord, Master, Savior — all at a rummage sale. Was this a coincidence, or God's perfect timing?

Recovered Memory

Bruce Stunkard

Do not remember the former things, or consider
the things of old. (v. 18)

I was a male glossophobiac. An avoider of spotlights. Stage frightened. Intensely afraid of speaking in public.

Throughout my high school and college years, any assignments requiring an oral presentation became a Gethsemane experience. Such public tasks became stomach churning, heart pumping, blood-sweating ordeals that drove me to fervent prayer: "O my Father, if it be possible, let this cup pass from me and if this cup may not pass away from me, give me the flu. In Jesus' name. Amen."

Without any aid from mental health specialists, I knew the origin of this social phobia — a sixth-grade poetry recital at Washburn Elementary School in Duluth, Minnesota.

In the fateful spring of 1963, my teacher, Mr. George Mead, told the class that we were going to have a poetry recital. To up the educational ante, we would be performing memorized poems from the elevated gymnasium stage before invited guests — our mothers. Now, I don't recall any anxiety with this assignment. Up to this point, I enjoyed the limelight. In fact, I'd regularly volunteered for any speaking parts at the Sunday School Christmas Program.

Mr. Mead informed us that we had a month to prepare. He provided our timetable: a week to select our poem, two weeks to memorize it, and a week for dress rehearsal, with the program on a Friday afternoon. As usual, I procrastinated till the day before we were to make our selection and headed to the local Carnegie Library. My selection process had two criteria — shortness and nothing girly. Those conditions were met by the twentieth century English Poet Laureate, John Masefield's, "Sea Fever." Three stanzas and a "lonely sea and sky." Coincidentally, his poem offered my pre-adolescent heart words to express my dreams of Lake Superior and a "gypsy life."

After turning in my poem selection, the tedious work of memorization was postponed until the weekend before our dress rehearsal. By Sunday evening, I was able to recite the poem. When my turn came at the dress rehearsal, I did all right, except for an occasional pause or two. Mr. Mead then pronounced the dress code — white blouses and black skirts for girls; white shirts, black bow ties, and pants for boys. His final word to us was get to bed early so we would be "up and at 'em."

On the day of the poetry recital, I remember experiencing irritability at the breakfast table and a curious gnawing in the pit of my stomach. At school, the air was ripe with excitement. The girls were chattering. Some were talking about being so scared they might forget or faint or wet their pants. Most of the boys had grown uncharacteristically silent. The boys who did speak employed the time honored male strategy of diversion, talking about baseball, bikes, or the Swiss Army knives they would be awarded at the Spring Banquet for being school crossing guards. I was in the "quiet camp," but unusually alert.

Then show time arrived. Mr. Mead had us line up in our order of appearance. I was near the end of the program, following a kid named Dave Timmons. Dave was a mystery to us. He was a round kid with an incomprehensible vocabulary. He spent half his time with us, and half time at a special school downtown for the "academically gifted." He hadn't been there for rehearsal. We entered the queue in order, making our way down the back stairs from our third floor classroom, passing the lunchroom with its lingering smell of milk carton, to the awaiting stage and an audience of mothers. To ease the tension, I asked Dave how he was doing. He surprised me with his candor. He said he hoped he wouldn't be an embarrassment to his mother. I hadn't thought about that possibility.

As each student made his stage debut, the line advanced two steps, until I was backstage. The place seemed so much brighter and more important than I had expected. While I struggled to make the adjustment, Dave's turn came. I watched him move directly to the microphone and introduce his poem — "Casey at the Bat, A

Ballad of the Republic" by Ernest L. Thayer. As he spoke the first line — "The outlook wasn't brilliant for the Mudville nine that day," something entered and transformed him before my eyes. He didn't recite the poem. The poem seemed to recite him, moving his body, raising and lowering his voice to match the action of its words.

Dave Timmons was possessed and his poetic possession mesmerized us to the very end — "and somewhere men are laughing (a howl of derision), and somewhere children shout (yippee!), but there is no joy in Mudville — mighty Casey has struck out (boooo!)." And then Dave hung his head in sympathy for the residents of Mudville and walked off stage right to a thundering round of applause seldom heard in the early 1960s.

That was when I learned about following the "hard act." Someone behind gave me a hiss and a push. I slowly walked to the microphone and felt I had just entered an unknown dimension.

Though the lights initially blinded me, I began — John Masefield's "Sea Fever."

> *I must go down to the seas again, to the lonely sea and*
> *   the sky,*
> *And all I ask is a tall ship and a star to steer her by,*
> *And the wheel's kick and the wind's song and the white*
> *   sail's shaking,*
> *And a grey mist on the sea's face, and a grey dawn*
> *   breaking.*
>
> *I must ...*

And there were no words to follow. I asked, searched, knocked for them, but I didn't receive, find, or have the door opened. Not knowing what else to do, I started over. "I must go down to the seas again, to the lonely sea and the sky." Again finding nothing at the end of the first stanza, but a vague memory of "grey mist" and a "grey dawn." It was then in the vast sea of anonymous women, my eyes locked on my mother. Her blue eyes were growing larger with each second of her son's dumbfoundedness. Her fear mobilized me. I knew what to do. I quickly started over and recited the first stanza for the third time. I didn't wait for the second stanza to arrive. I recited part of the third stanza and made up some words to rhyme with them. Then I walked off the stage.

It felt like a dream state. Everything seemed to slow down. I made my way up the stairs to my classroom. I sat at my old oak and wrought iron desk. I surrendered to gravity and lowered my forehead to the hinged top with my hands dangling at my side. Then wave after wave of hot, moist shame rolled through me. From that moment on, the word "failure" was written on my forehead so everyone could see.

For the next decade, whenever called to speak in public, I immediately recalled that story and was soon given another dunking in the baptismal waters of shame. As I stood before others to speak, they were changed into critics, mockers, judges. They weighed me in the balance and found me wanting. I had developed a full-blown case of glossophobia.

In my senior year of college, I experienced a spiritual renewal. My heart was warmed, like Wesley's, and I had a personal encounter with the Divine. I began attending an evangelical Christian church. About a year later, the pastor asked me to preach a Sunday evening sermon. Once again, the old, old story and its sea billows rolled. I said what many Christians say when buying time, "I'll pray about it."

I really did pray, asking the Lord for help. In fact, I fasted and prayed. One evening, several days into the fast, while in prayer, I lowered my forehead to my desk and entered into a dream or some altered state. I was back at Washburn Elementary in the spring of '63, observing a sixth grade boy at a microphone on an old gymnasium stage trying to remember the words to a poem. I watched the boy walk off the stage. He would not lift his head as he made his way to the back stairs. I smelled stale milk and wax. I followed him up the three flights to his classroom. I watched him put his forehead down on his desk as I anticipated the end of that very familiar story.

But to my surprise, that was not the end. As the boy flushed with shame, I heard the doorknob quietly turn. The door opened. Slow deliberate footsteps made their way beside the boy. All I could see were his scuffed black wingtips. He placed his hand on the boy's shoulder and spoke. "Don't be ashamed. You did good. It took real courage to keep trying as you did." The boy did not acknowledge his presence. There was a moment of silence. The man removed his hand, turned around, and shut the door behind him.

Then I raised my head from my desk. I realized that I had made a decision back then to reject an affirmation in favor of self-condemnation. In so doing, I had forgotten part of the story. In truth, I felt as though I had rejected the grace of God. I had cast out love and opened the door for fear to enter. As I pondered this recovered memory, I knew that I had just been given a divine gift. I was given the choice to let go of self-loathing and be healed. I could continue to be paralyzed by the fear of making mistakes, and avoid risk-taking, or accept a decade-old affirmation of encouragement and open my eyes to new possibilities. I chose to be healed. Two weeks later, I preached my first sermon. Now I am a circuit-riding Methodist preacher in a three-point charge and loving every opportunity to proclaim the precious message of God's healing word.

Dedicated to the unknown masculine soul with scuffed black wingtips.

Holy Week
And Easter

The mystic does not enter on his quest because he desires the happiness of the Beatific Vision, the ecstasy of union with the Absolute, or any other personal reward ... The true mystic claims no promises and makes no demands. He goes because he must ... knowing that for those who can live it, this alone is life.

Evelyn Underhill

Thomas S. Kepler, *The Evelyn Underhill Reader* (Nashville: Abingdon Press, 1962), p. 36.

A Single Drop Of Blood

Wayne Frank

"This cup that is poured out for you is the new covenant in my blood. But see, the one who betrays me is with me, and his hand is on the table. For the Son of Man is going as it has been determined, but woe to that one by whom he is betrayed!" (vv. 20b-22)

I was first elected as an Alderman on Milwaukee's south side after a special election in 1973. I was re-elected in 1976, and in 1979 I was certain I would be elected again in 1980. So, I formed a plan to run for President of the Common Council. In those days, the form of city government was a "strong council/weak mayor" system, but Mayor Henry Maier had forged a strong base of support within the Council, within City Departments, and with the voters. He would not tolerate an independent Council President, even though the position was not decided by him, but by a majority of the allegedly "independent" Aldermen.

I was easily elected to a third term. My hard work was paying off, and it was soon apparent that I had the votes needed to be elected President of the Common Council. In a straw vote, taken in public and traditionally binding, I was elected 16-0 by my colleagues. My biography and picture were in the newspapers and on television. Letters, wires, and phone calls of congratulations came in. The mayor knew he would no longer have complete control of the Common Council. My enemies needed little prompting. With only five days to go before the official vote, which was supposed to be *pro forma*, I was now losing support.

In those days, I was virtually a daily communicant at St. Matthew's Catholic Church on South 25th Street. I had been under a great deal of self-imposed pressure for over a year. Now the thought of my colleagues ignoring an election, that both the public and I thought I had won fairly, was almost unbearable. I developed an inadvertent twitch under one eye. I hyperventilated once. A friend who was close to the mayor, and who knew what was happening, left the city. On a Saturday morning, three days before the official vote, I received communion while feeling absolutely alone and betrayed. As I knelt, eyes closed, trying to pray, I could feel my heart pounding inside my chest as though it would explode from the pressure within. Then, in an indescribable instant, I was in another place. Dressed in a white robe, I found myself kneeling at the foot of a cross. Simultaneously, I was also over the right shoulder of the man on the cross, looking down and seeing myself below, kneeling, in great pain. In another instant, I was back in my body at the foot of the cross just as a small, single drop of blood fell and landed on my head. A wonderful, sweet peace began to flow through me from head to foot, as again, in another instant, I found myself back in church alongside my wife.

We walked home. All I could say to my wife was, "Something happened." A few blocks later I had to sit and try to explain what happened as the tears began to flow. Somehow I made it home, exhausted but at peace. Surprisingly, I had a peaceful day, but I knew my dream was collapsing all around me. I felt then, and I still feel now, that I suffered an injustice, but I believe God interceded to give me the strength to endure and to suffer in dignity. Why? To this day I still don't know why. Three days after this healing vision, the Common Council elected a so-called "compromise" President. Five or six years later, out of character for him, the mayor apologized for what had happened, and he offered me a high administrative job. I respectfully declined. But this story is not about me; it's about God, and 22 years later, I still haven't figured it out.

Maundy Thursday Visions

"For I have set you an example, that you also
should do as I have done to you. Very truly, I tell
you, servants are not greater than their master,
nor are messengers greater than the one who sent
them. If you know these things, you are blessed if
you do them." (vv. 15-17)

Lisa Lancaster

In 1985, I was struggling deeply with a very painful friendship. I was also at a time in my life where I was being overloaded with the "Christ suffered on the cross, so it is the calling of all Christians to suffer like him" sentiment. I could not make the distinction between the "cost of discipleship" and healthy self-care and self-love. Things in the friendship had come to a head for me one day. I was weeping and praying, saying, "God, I just can't do this any more! I can't stay in this friendship any more — it is tearing me apart!" Not coincidentally, this was Maundy Thursday, and I had just come from a worship service that told me more about Christ's suffering, and our call to suffer, again!

As soon as I cried out this prayer, I had an image of Christ on the cross, glaring down at me! And he said, "I'm hanging here — and you can't handle a little pain?" Almost immediately, I knew that this vision was a parody of how I had been seeing Jesus! I laughed and cried, knowing Jesus had sent me that vision to free me from my unhealthy perceptions of him. Because of my personality, I know that a vision of Jesus saying, "There, there," would never have had the same impact! Because of the vision, my spirituality and prayer life have been forever changed.

Sara Jan Garza

In January, 1978, my firstborn child, a son named Robin, died of crib death (SIDS) at the age of thirteen months. I was devastated and suicidal. I felt like my son was all alone and needed me. I went to the grave every day so that he wouldn't feel so alone.

A few months later, while trying to decided whether or not to use an overdose of pills to "follow" my son to the grave, I went to the Maundy Thursday service at my church. As I knelt at the altar rail to prayer, I felt the urge to open my eyes and look up.

There I saw my little boy, smiling, holding someone's hand. I was amazed to see him, and then more amazed when I heard someone's voice. I looked up and saw that it was none other than my Lord, Jesus, who was holding Robin's hand. Jesus said to me, "Why are you so worried about your son? He is my son too, and I am with him. I will take care of him for you."

I have never stopped missing him, but I have the peace of knowing that Robin no longer needs me; he is well taken care of.

Is It Possible To Forgive After Murder?

Aba Gayle

*Then Jesus said, "Father, forgive them; for they
do not know what they are doing."* (v. 34a)

The first time I walked into the visiting room for death row inmates at San Quentin State Prison was the most frightening experience of my life. I had never had any experience with prison and had never known anyone who had been either a prisoner or prison employee. I knew what I had heard on the radio, been told by politicians, and seen on television and in the movies. I was not prepared for what I saw that day. I looked around the visiting room for condemned inmates and did not see a single monster. I saw perfectly ordinary men who were neatly dressed. They were seated with their wives, children, grandmothers, spiritual counselors, and friends. In fact, everywhere I looked, I saw the face of God! I was there to visit with the man who murdered my daughter, Catherine. She was nineteen when she died. It had been a long and difficult journey to the San Quentin Condemned visiting room.

That journey began with a terrible phone call telling me Catherine was dead: murdered. I began a dark trip of anger, rage, and lust for revenge that lasted for eight years. The district attorney assured me that he would find the man who committed this crime, convict him, and see him sentenced to death. He told me that when the man was executed I would find the healing and peace I needed. I had no spiritual faith at that time and I believed him. This promise of healing after an execution is the "magic bullet" offered to murder victims' families all over the United States by self-serving district attorneys. Even though he kept his promises and put a man on death row for my daughter's murder, eight years is too long a time to be consumed with hatred.

I was finally awakened to the truth by lessons I learned in Unity Church, the Church of Religious Science, years of intense study of all religious faiths, and becoming a student of *A Course in Miracles*. One night, after four years of study and prayer, a voice came to me. It said, "You must forgive him and you must let him know!" That voice was so loud and clear that I couldn't sleep that night. It had me out of bed at 4:00 a.m., at which time I found myself typing a letter to the man I had hated for so long: the man who murdered Catherine.

In the letter, I told him of the pain I had suffered and how unbearable it had been to lose Catherine. I also told him of the wonderful teachers who had come into my life and that I had come to know that I was able to forgive him. I explained that this did not mean that I felt he was innocent. I told him, "The Christ in me sends blessings to the Christ in you." The act of mailing the letter was a profound event of healing. The instant the letter went into the mailbox all of my anger, rage, and need for revenge simply disappeared, and in its place I was filled with love, peace, and joy. I was truly in a state of grace.

I received a letter back that expressed great joy that I had found such wonderful teachers who helped heal my pain. It also expressed the agony of knowing how deeply he had hurt so many people, especially Catherine's mother. He said it was more than his soul could bear. He thanked me for the opportunity to write and express his remorse. He enclosed a visitor's form. It took ninety days for me to get permission from the prison to visit.

Today, I continue to visit San Quentin Death Row. I am totally opposed to the death penalty for any reason. I know that a state sanctioned, premeditated murder will not bring back my daughter. I know that an execution does nothing to honor her memory.

I also know this: forgiveness heals. Forgiveness gave me back my life. Forgiveness is a gift you give yourself.

Chosen As Witnesses

They put him to death by hanging him on a tree;
but God raised him on the third day and allowed
him to appear, not to all the people but to us who
were chosen by God as witnesses, and who ate
and drank with him after he rose from the dead.
(vv. 39b-41)

Theonia Amenda

Our first grandchild died two months shy of his fourth birthday. Chad was a beautiful little boy who was severely handicapped, unable to walk or talk, and fed most of his short life through a tube connected to his stomach through his abdominal wall. He was also given four medications to control seizures. Chad could smile and laugh, though, and did that whenever anyone paid attention to him.

At Chad's funeral service, I shared that I truly believed that, in death, Chad's little body was whole again: he could now do all that he could not do in his lifetime.

The day after we laid his little body to rest, I had to fly to Nashville for a five-day event for which I, along with four other team members, had leadership responsibilities. During that week, I had two visions of Chad — both at times my heart and mind were not dwelling on him or my sorrow.

The first day, as I was sitting in a classroom listening to a lecture, I glanced away from the lecturer for a moment and saw Chad standing and smiling at me. He was there and gone in a blink of an eye, leaving me to wonder if I had really seen him or just imagined him.

Several days later I was at worship, coming out of prayer and focusing on the chalice and the bread on the communion table.

111

Again, momentarily, there was Chad. This time he was on his tip-toes, reaching up for some bread as he turned and sheepishly smiled at his grandmother. Again I disbelieved what I was seeing.

Later I shared with the leadership team what I had experienced and asked them if they felt my mind had created those visions, even though I was not dwelling on Chad at those times. As they responded to me, I came to realize that it didn't matter; I didn't have to understand what happened. I was given a gift: two visions showing me that what I truly believed was really so. Later, I shared my experiences with the rest of the family, including our daughter, Chad's mother, and saw how comforting it was for them to hear it.

I have never had such an experience before or since, nor have I ever doubted, after sharing with others that day, that what I saw was real. It was a gift I was given for some reason that I do not understand, but for which I am still grateful.

Lee Meissner

John was in his early eighties and was living in a nursing home because his wife couldn't care for him at home. His only problem was that, because of the loss of a leg, he had trouble getting around. And, for some unknown reason, he was getting weaker. His mind was as good as ever.

While he was in the nursing home, John's sister, who lived about 100 miles away, died. She died during the night and John's wife was notified early the next morning. She called me, her pastor, to go with her to tell John, because she didn't know how he would take the news. She wasn't sure how to tell him, but she knew that the pastor would know just the right words.

We entered his room at about 9:00 a.m. He had had breakfast and was feeling as well as possible. We began with the usual small talk, and then John said, "You came to tell me that my sister died last night." John's wife was stunned, but I was more interested in how he knew.

John said that his sister had come to his room during the night. She told him that it was her time to leave and she wanted to say good-bye. She wanted to tell him that she was okay.

Before leaving the nursing home, I asked the head nurse if anyone had called to tell John of the death of his sister. No one had called. John could only have known because he saw his sister, as he said.

Holy Coincidences

Now Jesus did many other signs in the presence of his disciples, which are not written in this book.
(v. 30)

Lee Domann

My mother's only brother died in March, 1983, in a car/train accident. I was devastated. Uncle Bud was like a father, a brother, and a best friend to me. He had visited my family and me in Nashville only the week before. It was a sad drive I made back to Kansas, and an even sadder funeral.

That night, I sat with my mother as she entered Uncle Bud's name in the birth/death section of the old family Bible. As we read the names, we were suddenly startled by something we'd never noticed before. The number *11* was all over the page — literally. Numerous relatives had been born on or had died on the eleventh day of any given month. My mother's birth date was September 11, my son's January 11. A surprising number had been born in November, the eleventh month of the year. A number of them, including my father, had been born in 1911.

We also noted a preponderance of *22*s, a multiple of *11*. My father, for instance, was born on September 22. His mother had died on June 22.

While my mother was intrigued by this phenomenon, I was emotionally shaken. When I went to bed later that evening, my mind was whirling with fresh memories of similar occurrences from the trip I had just taken to Kansas two days before. I had traveled only a few miles from Nashville when I began to notice *11* popping up frequently enough to catch my attention.

Once or twice when I had stopped at a service station to fill up with gas, the amount of purchase had contained an *11*. As I recall, one time the amount was actually $11.11. The pump had stopped at that amount when the tank was full.

As I drove I would occasionally look at my watch or the clock above the radio. Eerily, the time frequently would be eleven minutes before or after the hour. When I stopped at a motel for the night, the desk clerk handed me the room key and said, "Have a restful sleep. You're in Room 11."

In the coming months, I found all of this to be enormously comforting as the marvel continued, though not as frequently. When it did happen, I felt a warmth, a closeness to Bud, and an assurance that he was just fine on The Other Side. I don't know what the significance of *11* is, or how it fits into my spiritual journey as one who is trying to follow Jesus. A numerologist has told me that *11* is, in her words, "a very high spiritual number." I don't know what she means. But I do believe that the God Jesus came to tell us about loves us so much that he/she will use anything to reassure us that all is well in ways we can't see in this lifetime. If the repetition of a numeral is what it takes to get my attention, then that's the tool God will use.

Weeks later, after Uncle Bud's funeral, I went back to visit his gravesite. I had to laugh out loud. I shook my head in amazement as I noted that on every grave marker adjacent to his resting place, there appears the number *11*.

Thanks be to God for signs and wonders that comfort, assure, and encourage us.

Bill Hoglund

Back in the days of my hospital chaplaincy, assigned to what was then a newly-opened retirement center connected to the hospital by a tunnel, I felt I always had the best of both worlds in my ministry. When I needed to "decompress" after some tough situation at the hospital, there were always the appreciative seniors at the retirement center, where my "boss," himself a retired clergyman, had carved an office for me out of what was originally intended to be a janitor's storage closet.

Charlie and Doris were an older couple in the building who had come from New Jersey. A native Midwesterner, I always got a kick out of their thick Jersey accents. I appreciated them both, but Charlie loved to regale me with golf stories from his career in sales. Many a deal was consummated on the course, and he must have been a pretty fair golfer in his day.

Quite some time later, when I heard things had gone bad for him after a stay in the hospital with pneumonia, I hurried up to the Intensive Care Unit to be with him and his wife. We shared precious moments and prayers before he gently passed on to what he'd once referred to hopefully as his ultimate "promotion."

Getting into the '67 Chevy Impala I drove, later on that cool, crisp night, I noticed the clock of my battered ol' beater had stopped at 8:28. I didn't give it a second thought since the clock and everything else in the car seemed to have a mind of its own. But the next morning, before her children gathered around her from different parts of the country, I received a phone call from Doris. "Reverend Bill, I know Charlie's okay. I just know it," she said calmly and without tears. "You see, the clock above our kitchen table stopped last night. That clock was a wedding present and it has traveled all over the country with us. It stopped at exactly the same time the doctor said he 'officially' passed away, 8:28 p.m."

You cannot tell me that this was a coincidence, for "Christ has prepared a place for us" (John 3). Doris and I know Charlie's there, peacefully "promoted," maybe "wheeling and dealing" with the saints on some celestial golf course!

Britney-Lee Joy Hessel

One Saturday, I was babysitting. My sister Shawna was playing in her room, and I was sitting with my back against the wall and a blanket pulled up to my shoulders. I was really sleepy. The first time I nodded off, something that felt like a large hand pushed my left cheek gently, but hard enough to wake me up. I looked at Shawna, but she wasn't even close to me. The same thing happened two more times.

116

After the third time, I asked Shawna if she touched me, and she said no. I was a little freaked out! I realized that God was keeping me awake so that I wouldn't get in trouble. He knew that I couldn't really take care of my sister if I was asleep. I had been praying that God would help me, my brother, and my sister stay out of trouble. It's really great to know that he is there for me, and everybody else in the world.

Debra Partridge

After my father passed away, I inherited the daily diaries that my mother had kept from the time I was three years old. It was totally amazing to me that she found time to write in a diary, since she worked full time and raised six kids. I learned so much about her and our family from reading them.

When my grandfather, James Archie Sumwalt, was sick in March of 1961, Mother wrote, "Dad is not good." On March 7, she wrote that Grandpa was worse. My father, James Allen Sumwalt, got the call from Grandma later that day that he was gone.

That night, my dad drove over sixty miles, from Madison to Richland Center in southwest Wisconsin, in a blinding blizzard. Mother didn't want him to go alone, but he was determined to be with his family. She wrote in her diary that Dad's trip to Richland Center was pretty scary. Visibility was so bad that the only way he could tell if he was on the road was to keep the car door open. Thank God that he made it. He also drove home the next day to help mother get six children packed and ready to go back for the funeral. I don't remember much from that time, but I do remember how confused I felt when I saw my daddy, the big man in my life, break down in tears.

Life went on and time went by, and then one day it happened all over again.

My father became ill around Thanksgiving time in 1992. In December, they found an aneurysm on the back side of an artery to his heart. Surgery was successful, but during his recovery the doctors discovered cancer in his kidneys, one totally gone and the other

117

almost. He got better for a little while, and then in January he just got down and could never get back up.

Dad was living in Florida, where he and Mother had retired after leaving Wisconsin. We were living in Alabama, and my husband and I would travel every weekend to visit with Dad in the hospital. It was very hard to see him so sick. He was able to hang on until he saw each of his six children one last time. My brother Dan, from Wisconsin, made it down on the third of March. Dad lost the battle with cancer on March 7, 1993, 32 years to the day after his father's death.

My parents wished to be buried in Madison, so arrangements were made and Dad's body was sent "home" to Wisconsin to be buried next to Mother. My sister, Diane, and her daughter drove to my home in Alabama and we all drove together to Wisconsin. We drove eighteen hours through a blinding blizzard. In Illinois, visibility was almost zero. We didn't even know when we crossed into Wisconsin. But when it got too bad, my husband said, "We have to pull off at the next exit no matter where it is." We were able to see a bright light off the side of the road and he said, "That's where we will go." When we took the exit off the highway, we were amazed to discover that it was exactly the exit we needed to get to Madison.

I have always believed that guardian angels gave us the light to find our way through the storm that night, just as they helped my father find his way when his father died so many years ago.

The Other End Of The Barrel

Shirley Lochowitz

But the Lord said to him, "Go, for he is an instru-
ment whom I have chosen to bring my name be-
fore Gentiles and kings and before the people of
Israel...." (v. 15)

Seven years ago, I was working as a police officer for the Town of Caledonia Police Department. On August 10, 1995, I was dispatched to a shooting call, only to learn on the way that the twelve-year-old boy who had been shot was my son. He had been shot by his fourteen-year-old friend, who had been playing with a .22 rifle that his father had allowed him to keep loaded under his bed.

I was the first one on the scene. As I walked into the back of the house, I saw my son, Nick, sitting against the frame of the basement doorway. He had been shot in the stomach. I thought my son was going to die in front of me, that's how bad he looked.

After almost five hours of emergency surgery, my son was given only a fifty percent chance of living, because he had lost so much blood. Although I didn't know it at the time, this was a moment in which my whole life would be changed forever.

My son was in the hospital for a full week. He was very weak and he had lost a lot of weight. Things went smoothly for a while. Nick tried to get right back to normal, but I was so afraid for him that I remember, when he would fall asleep on the couch, I used to just stare at him. I could only be reassured that he was okay by seeing his chest rise and fall. I was so grateful to see that he was still breathing!

As time went on, my fears grew and grew. I decided that there was no way I could go back to police work, although, after almost fourteen years, my love for it was deep. But my fears were turning into panic attacks as my world grew smaller and smaller. I started having terrible nightmares about the shooting. I could not sleep or eat and I withdrew more and more. I could not face the people I worked with for fear that they would find me weak for not being able to return to police work. I found that alcohol took away the fear, helped me to sleep, and made me better able to cope. But soon even that didn't work. I was constantly overcome with fear — dread — of something terrible happening.

I now know, looking back, that I was extremely depressed. My whole world that I had known before the shooting was gone. It was not a safe place, and I was *not* in control, as I had thought so many times. Then, instead of taking the fear away, the alcohol made it worse. I needed help. It wasn't until I found a wonderful doctor that I was able to understand that these were truly symptoms of post traumatic stress. What I saw when I walked into that home on that day jolted my soul onto a path where I never thought I would go.

I had been raised Catholic, but for many years I had questioned my faith. Where was God? How could I get to know him? Well, that has been the blessing of this shooting. It is how I truly came to know that God is always with me, sending me his love as I send it back to him.

You see, a short time after the shooting, I started speaking out on the issue of safe gun storage. I have dedicated myself to educating others about how important it is, if you have a gun in your home, to keep it secured so that these types of shootings don't keep happening. Needless to say, it was not a very popular subject seven years ago. No one wanted to listen. But I have seen dramatic changes over the last few years. There have been many times when I have just wanted to quit, believing no one wanted to hear what I had to say. But then, one night I had a vision that changed my life.

I had gone to sleep and I found myself in a very dark spot, standing on the blacktop of my grade school parking lot, which is also the parking lot of the church. It was a sunny day, but suddenly it grew very, very, dark with what looked like storm clouds, until it was pitch black. I was standing in complete darkness feeling full of fear. Then there was a small break in the clouds. As they began to part, a bright, rainbow-filled, glorious light came down and shone directly on me. Then a large, strong voice said, "Our Father is very proud of you." I am not sure whose voice it was ... maybe Jesus or an angel ... but at that moment I was enveloped in love, calmness, peace. If I close my eyes I can still feel it today. I woke up with a sense of *knowing* that God is with me and that this was the work I was to continue.

This happened a few years ago, but I have no doubt that I was spoken to, and I am convinced that this shooting happened for a reason. I am living out that reason by sharing our story and the message of safe gun storage. There have still been times when I have doubted and have asked God for a sign and he has always, always come through. When I think of giving up, I say to God, "Please, if you want me to continue, send me something," and the phone will ring that day or the next with someone looking for me to speak on safe gun storage. Even my husband said to me, "Geez, how many times do you need to be shown?"

My experience truly makes my belief that all things happen in divine order, and in their own time, stronger. May God also bring you light and love.

Life-giving Plasma

Harold Weaver

Yea, though I walk through the valley of the shadow
of death, I will fear no evil; for thou art with me;
thy rod and thy staff — they comfort me. (v. 4 KJV)

In August of 1966, I visited Germany. As we traveled, I discovered that we were only twelve miles from a place where I had been stationed during World War II, so we drove over to Geilenkircken. What a thrilling difference there was! The last time I had seen Geilenkircken was when the streets were churned into mud by tanks and trucks. GIs lived in the houses. I saw the house I had lived in, and one block down the street was a schoolhouse where wounded soldiers, brought back from the front lines, were taken. There's one incident that took place in that schoolhouse-turned-hospital that I will never forget.

Shortly after midnight, on an utterly black night, a Jewish doctor sent a messenger to the house I was living in because he wanted a Protestant chaplain. I was asleep, but dressed, and went in a hurry with the sergeant who had called in his jeep. A young soldier was lying on the table in the basement of the schoolhouse. He had been wounded and was suffering from severe shock. Because of the shock, his blood vessels had become flabby; it was impossible to inject the life-giving plasma into his body, although repeated attempts had been made. There was no hope for him, and therefore the medic thought we should have prayer.

So, the few of us there bowed our heads for a moment and then I began to repeat Psalm 23. Something happened that I had heard of, but never seen. Just as we came to the passage, "Yea though I walk through the valley of the shadow of death, I will fear no evil, for thou art with me," it was noticed that the soldier's lips were moving. The doctor interrupted and asked the youth his name. His eyelids fluttered and he whispered his name and serial number. I had not known until then that he had lost his dog tags. He would have died an unknown soldier.

The marvelous thing that happened was that this lad's blood vessels began to regain their resiliency, which permitted the blood plasma to be introduced. His arm was later amputated, but he lived! Somewhere today, there is a one-armed Lutheran veteran who does not know that his life was saved because he knew the Twenty-third Psalm.

The thing that struck me most about that young man was that, in his early years, he had been brought up to know Psalm 23 and the Lord's Prayer. The familiar and beautiful old religious truths had reached down into his subconscious mind and they became the hands of God to bring him to life again.

Editor's Note: This personal story is from a sermon titled, "Thatch Your Roof In Warm Weather," which Dr. Harold Weaver preached at Wauwatosa Avenue United Methodist Church in Milwaukee, Wisconsin, June 4, 1967. Dr. Harold Weaver was one of my predecessors in the Wauwatosa Avenue pulpit and one of my heroes. He was a gentle, loving man who spoke out fervently for open housing and equal rights. Dr. Weaver died on May 26, 2002, at the age of 87, after a long, distinguished career as a pastor in United Methodist Churches in Ohio and Wisconsin.

A Call To Ministry

Nancy Nichols

"I also heard a voice saying to me, 'Get up, Peter; kill and eat.' But I replied, 'By no means, Lord; for nothing profane or unclean ever entered my mouth.' But a second time the voice answered from heaven, 'What God has made clean, you must not call profane.'" (vv. 7-9)

I joined the church when I was in junior high school. Part of the confirmation class included preparing a worship service as a group. We passed a black hat around and each confirmand pulled out a slip of paper assigning the role each person would play in the service. The slip of paper I pulled said "sermon." I was twelve. I don't remember if there was any controversy that I got the sermon role. I do remember that I shared that responsibility with another person, a boy. Was that in the original plan? I don't know.

After confirmation, I was often the layperson who led the congregation through worship. I continued to go to youth group, outside Bible studies, and Sunday school. However, I never found my way into any kind of leadership in those organizations. I did not preach another sermon until I had completed my first year of seminary. I was a useful participant, one who could be counted on to support the leaders, listen to the others in the group, and play my guitar during group singing. In short, I fulfilled my role expectations as a nice, sweet, supportive girl!

In hindsight, it is obvious that my life was being shaped by my desire to be involved in the church in more than a surface capacity. I do not recall anyone ever mentioning that I should consider ministry as a possibility for my life. It was assumed, at least by me, that I would follow along in the family tradition of education and prepare to become a teacher. I do know that, had anyone suggested ministry, I would have said no. I had never seen a clergy woman, did not know that women could be ministers, and was influenced, at least to some degree, by friends who believed that women should be silent in the church and by a society that was just shifting toward supporting educated women who made lifestyle choices that did not fall into the traditional roles of secretary, store clerk, nurse, teacher, or marriage soon after high school.

During my senior year of college, I dropped out of secondary education. I finished with a BA in History. I was not prepared to do anything and I knew it. I had spent my last semester of college in Chicago doing an Urban Studies experience. During that semester, my entire world turned upside down. I examined my assumptions of what it meant to be middle class, what it meant to be white, and most of all, what it meant to be woman. I began to realize that, although there were social limitations, I could be more than wife, mother, and teacher. The path was being laid for me to accept my call to ministry. The year was 1980.

After I graduated from college, I went back home for a while. As always, my connection to the church was strong: I attended worship, chaperoned youth groups, went to Sunday school. The minister, who had come while I was in college, began talking to me about going into the ministry. I kept saying no. He introduced me to a woman who was serving a nearby United Methodist church while attending seminary. My ears perked up, but I said no. Finally, probably more to shut him up than for any other reason, something I still remind him of on a regular basis, I decided to go to seminary: for the education, not to be a minister. By spring of my first year, I realized that I was, indeed, called into the parish ministry, and started the process toward ordination. The time frame, from confirmation to my entrance into seminary, was ten years.

Would this decision have been any easier had I been male? I don't know that the decision to enter professional ministry is ever easy, but I think it would have been suggested much earlier in my life had I been a boy-child rather than a girl-child. I know I would have had more opportunities in college to explore leadership roles within the church body had I been male, and I suspect that even leadership in my home youth group would have been easier had I been a boy. I do know that the idea of being a minister would not have been as foreign to me had I been male — I would have at least looked and sounded like all the other ministers who had crossed my path. I wasn't just struggling with the decision to become a full-time, ordained minister. I was struggling to do something that few women were doing at that time and I didn't perceive myself as either a rebel or a pioneer.

The struggle I had accepting my call to ministry did not end with my decision to pursue ordination. If anything, it became harder. Never did anyone in my family discourage me from the path toward ordination, nor did anyone in my home church. However, when I was recommended for ministry by the local personnel committee, I reminded them that by recommending me it meant they, in essence, were saying they would welcome the appointment of a woman as their minister. I was met with less than accepting gazes.

When I finished seminary and went to my first church, I was, like most young professionals, unprepared for making the transition from school to practice. In other words, I had no clue of what I was supposed to be doing. I remember staring at an empty desk and asking myself, "What now?" I was not successful. My first several years in ministry were miserable. I often thought about quitting, but for some reason I could not. I still believed that I had something to offer the church, and that God was calling me to be there. I tried to find women who could mentor me, but few had much more experience than I did. I did find some wonderful clergymen who walked with me during those difficult early years, and helped me identify the one thing I was unwilling so see, that many (not all) of my struggles were connected to my gender. I made many of the same mistakes that many clergymen who are new in ministry make. In my case, my gender was blamed. In theirs, it was inexperience. I didn't want to accept that. I wanted to take full responsibility for my failures, but in the final analysis, I had to name the sexism that was limiting my professional success and personal happiness.

In The United Methodist Church, the Bishop appoints clergy to local churches after discussion with the Cabinet; a group of clergy called District Superintendents who are given administrative oversight in a geographical area. The common practice is for churches to accept the person appointed by the Bishop. Two years after I left seminary I was taken to the Pastor Parish committee of one church by the Superintendent and introduced as their new pastor. They turned me down. They liked me "as a person," but were sure that, because I was a woman, their congregation would revolt and they would lose members. They also did not want to lose face in the small, conservative town where they were located. One member on that committee was a distant cousin, who had known both my mother and my grandmother. She apologized for the committee's decision, but supported it. I found out later that the youth from that church went to the Pastor Parish committee and told the adults they were disappointed in them! It truly was against the United Methodist polity for this to happen, but it did. I was stuck. I had to have a place to be, and there were no more openings. I clung to the scripture that promises God will not leave you orphaned. I felt very much alone, although I had the support of family and friends. I learned, at a deeper level than I had ever known before, to trust in God!

When I was finally ordained as an Elder, five years after I left seminary, I felt that I had arrived. I was appointed to be an associate at a large, downtown church. I had met the senior pastor and knew I could work with him. However, within weeks of my arrival, a local person placed the following message on a public sign: "Women ministers, totally unscriptural, shame on the Methodists." While this man was not a member of my congregation, I could not help but believe he represented at least one perspective present in the parish. Later, my father told me that, when he attended worship on my first Sunday there, he overheard someone say, "Well, I suppose we were going have to get one someday; might as well get it over with." I can only imagine what the response would have been if I had been appointed as the senior pastor! Once again, before I could even show what I could do, I had to defend my right to do it!

Much of my work in that congregation ended up centered on youth ministry, although that was not the original plan. I hated youth ministry! I liked the kids, but I didn't know how to work with them. In hindsight, I know that some of my struggles had to do with the way they, the youth, felt about women. Many of them came from families where their mothers did not work outside of the home. If they did, it was in the traditional jobs of teaching, social work, nursing, and secretarial. I was paving the way, not only for myself but also for a generation of youth who still were uncomfortable with the idea of a woman in ministry.

It was just at this time, when I was ready to give up, that I remembered an event from that long-ago spring when I was confirmed. I was sitting under a tree, thinking about preaching on the Lord's Prayer, when I clearly heard a voice say, "Nancy, be a minister." And I responded, "No, God, women don't do that." It had taken twenty years for me to remember my initial call to ministry. I forgot. God did not.

God's Prodding Fork

Kay Boone Stewart

During the night Paul had a vision: there stood a
man of Macedonia pleading with him and saying,
"Come over to Macedonia and help us." When he
had seen the vision, we immediately tried to cross
over to Macedonia, being convinced that God had
called us to proclaim the good news to them. (vv.
9-10)

A silver dining fork hangs against dark blue, crushed velvet in an antique, gold box frame in my office. Often, my eye rests on it. John, a friend visiting from California, asked me one day what it represented.

"It is my prodding fork," I told him.

His eyes twinkled with curiosity. We sat down for dinner and I told him and his wife Joyce this story:

I believe in angels. If I had ever had any doubts, they were all put to rest one spring day in 1979.

The closing luncheon of my Bible study class was being held at my home. In addition, I had been asked to choose a gift from the class for our leader. My week had been unusually demanding, and now there was only one day left to prepare the house, shop for food, and select the gift.

The Lord has been faithful in helping me find just the right item for some need or person. Entering traffic, I prayed for direction. Receiving an inward message, I proceeded to the mall, parked my car, and chose the first entrance to the department store.

My eyes were greeted by racks of women's blouses, ranked by color. Since the group had agreed on a personal gift, I checked the selection. Soon, I came upon a long-sleeved, feminine blouse in crème. Her color. Her style. I purchased it and took it to the wrapping station, grateful for the speedy solution. But while waiting for it to be wrapped, another inward message came to me to go to another store.

I argued inwardly with that suggestion, since my shopping was done and the suggested store was at the other end of the mall. Then, remembering that I had found a sale on my china and crystal at that store one day "by chance," I decided to investigate. The clerk agreed to finish my package and hold it until I returned.

I walked to the store at the other end of the mall. Once inside, I stood uncertainly for a few moments. No message came to guide me. My motto has always been, "If in doubt, go to lunch." It was early for lunch, but I went upstairs to the tearoom counter and sat down.

My order was taken immediately. Sipping a glass of water, I watched several people come and go. My meal was delayed, but I didn't press the issue because the puzzle of my errand had not yet unraveled. While waiting, I prayed silently for the counter occupants.

"Haven't you been served?" my waitress asked when she saw me, after some time, sitting with only water. I replied that I hadn't and she scurried away to reorder my food. The counter had emptied. I was alone.

A young, sleek-suited woman sat down opposite me in the next counter island. She was carrying a clipboard, which she wrote on while awaiting her order. I began praying for her, as I had for the others, careful not to watch her as I prayed. But I managed a good look at her face as she glanced up from her work, eyeing me once or twice. I was struck by her eyes. She appeared under some great strain, emotional, physical or spiritual, and her eyes, darkened and weary, showed it.

Our food arrived at the same time. I finished first, and I felt I must hasten back to the other end of the mall to retrieve the gift as my agenda beckoned. Praying must have been my mission, I reasoned. Then the inner voice said, "Tell her about me. Ask if she knows Jesus Christ." I panicked!

I had witnessed people in such conversations many times at airports and other public places, but I had never walked up to a stranger and said, "Do you know Jesus Christ?" It didn't seem right, somehow, like an invasion of privacy. Yellow to the core, I fled to the restroom. Rifling through my handbag, I looked for a tract or something that would do the job for me. I had cleaned out the bag the day before, and I knew I didn't have any such thing left, but I upended the bag on a table just to be sure. Nothing!

When I returned to the tearoom, she had left. Feeling a great relief, I started back to the first store, walking outside in the spring sunlight. Perhaps I would see a store that sold Christian literature. It was another dodge on my part, as I knew there was none on that street. Well, I told myself, I had probably misunderstood the directive, anyway, and now I had to hurry.

Suddenly I realized I wasn't making much progress toward the other end of the mall. I felt as if I was walking in deep snow. The going was slow and laborious and my breath was coming hard. I felt like I was being physically restrained!

How this appeared to passersby I don't know, as I seemed to be the only one aware of my predicament. I felt like I was in a time warp or something. "Go back!" was the message I kept hearing within. I argued with it. "Send someone else. I don't know what to do!" The reply was, "Go back! There *is* no one else!" Could I be the only obedient follower available in the crowd?

Obedient? As I entered the store, still bent on *my* errand, my own disobedience confronted me. I acknowledged it, but felt the Lord should understand *my* pressures of the day. As I reached the wrapping station, I struck a bargain with the Lord: "I will go back, but you must give me a pressing reason to go." I cringed, now, at the audacity layered on top of disobedience.

As I reached into my purse for a pen to sign for the parcel, my hand struck metal. Pulling it out, I found not a pen, but a fork! And it still had bits of food on the tines: warm food, not food from my lunch. Could it have dropped into my purse from the counter? No! I had totally emptied my purse in the restroom! I stared at the object in my hand, my heart beating like a trip hammer!

"Is something wrong?" the girl asked as she handed me the wrapped package in a bag.

"Oh — no!" I stammered, "I just can't find my pen." I stuffed the fork back into my purse and used the pen she gave me.

Returning to the other end of the mall as fast as my wobbly legs would carry me, I asked the Lord how to proceed. I was told the message she was to receive, and I ducked into the restroom and wrote it at the bottom of my grocery list and tore it off.

My next stop was the lunch counter, to return the fork. Embarrassed, I approached my waitress, telling her that I didn't know how the fork got into my purse, but it must have dropped off the counter. I was Peter, walking on water one moment and drowning in the waves the next.

"No, it isn't our pattern," she said, refusing to take it. I looked at the flatware on the counter. All of it matched, and none of it looked like the fork I held. I was being forced to keep it!

I asked her where the young woman I had seen at the counter worked. "Coats. Downstairs," she replied, glad to be rid of me.

The coat department silently bulged with coats. The young woman stood with her back to me, behind the register. For the second time that day we were alone. "Miss?" I asked tentatively, swallowing a lump in my throat. She turned and smiled at me, sweetly, but her eyes were still darkly burdened.

"You must be a very important person," I smiled shakily. "I was sent back to give you this." I handed her the note. She began to read silently:

> *The Lord Jesus Christ loves you. If you will turn your life over to him, he will handle everything for you. He will change your life. Amen.*

I had signed it with a cross instead of my name.

Knowing I had done my part (and that the angel would keep me rooted to the spot if I hadn't!), I turned and walked away. I didn't look back, but I felt a tremendous release. My angel escort whisked me through green traffic lights, grocery shopping, and housecleaning in record time. A round-eyed luncheon group heard my story the next day, as have many luncheon groups since.

Curiosity drove me back to the coat department of that store many times before I moved away from that California city, but I never saw the young woman again. I am sure time was running out for her in some way. It could have been the last opportunity for her to receive the invitation of the Lord into her life, or her last day on earth! That day, that moment, were crucial ones for her, I am certain. And to think, I almost walked away! How many times has my disobedience been a stumbling block for someone?

I am grateful for my "prodding fork," for with it the Lord prodded me into returning to the scene of need. It was the only time I was given such graphic evidence of his intentions. I will never forget the day the angel, the girl, and the fork made God very real to me.

The Lord is closer to us than breathing. Yes, he is! He is also the Hound of Heaven!

Don't Just Stand There!

Judith M. Evenden

*When he had said this, as they were watching, he
was lifted up, and a cloud took him out of their
sight. While he was going and they were gazing
up toward heaven, suddenly two men in white robes
stood by them. (vv. 9-10)*

It happened thirty years ago. I am standing at the graveside of
my grandmother, my father's mother. Many say her death is a blessing. After all, she has been sick for many years, a victim of that
dreaded disease, Alzheimer's, which steals away our loved ones,
one memory at a time. As this is my first funeral and as I am a
young teenager, I am unsure of how to act, where to stand, what to
feel.

In the Salvation Army, the faith family of my parents and all of
my grandparents, the tradition in which I have been raised, death is
viewed as a "Promotion." At death, one is considered to have been
"Promoted to Glory." Knowing this, I am uncertain that I can be
sad on such an occasion, although sadness fills my heart.

Rather than standing directly beside the grave for the commit-
tal service, I choose to stand back a little, by myself, hiding behind
my sunglasses. At the moment in which the final words are spoken
— earth to earth, ashes to ashes, dust to dust — my attention is
drawn upward, toward the sky. With my head tilted back, eyes looking up, I watch as the dark clouds part and a single gull flies up
through the opening into the bright sun. With the sight of this gentle,
soaring creature, a smile comes over my face and tears well up
behind my dark glasses.

I look back down at her grave. The beam of the sun is now
shining directly upon her casket. I glance around at the others; all

their eyes are cast down. Am I the only one to witness the accession of one whose body has died, but whose spirit is being lifted beyond the bonds of death? It is as though she has, in this moment, risen from the cold embrace of the grave and soared up into the loving arms of God.

Pentecost

"Behold him, a sacred voice is calling you.
All over the sky a sacred voice is calling you."

Black Elk

Marie Therese Archambault, *Black Elk: Living in the Sacred Hoop* (Cincinnati: St. Anthony Messenger Press, 1989), p. 17.

A Day Of Pentecost

Ellen Sherry

Divided tongues, as of fire, appeared among them,
and a tongue rested on each of them. (v. 3)

I was raised in the Congregational Church. I was baptized, went to Sunday school, was confirmed, and attended church regularly until I was in my late teens. However, church didn't mean anything to me and I didn't feel I got anything out of it, or feel connected to it in any way, so once I was away from home, I no longer attended services.

Prayer was pretty infrequent for me, but occasionally, when I would wake up worrying in the middle of the night, I would pray. Some of those prayers were answered, sometimes in rather dramatic ways. They were always selfish prayers, often having to do with the weather or other petty wants of mine. One night in December of 2000, I was thanking God for a prayer that had been answered. I said, "Thank you God, you're the greatest." And all of a sudden, a wide band of bright, white light came down at me from near the ceiling. My first thought was, "Oh, my gosh, this is going to hurt." But it didn't hurt, the light flowed into my chest and all I felt was some slight pressure. The light flowed and flowed into me, filling my heart to overflowing with indescribable love. It was the most amazing feeling; such a wonderful feeling of peace filled me — peace like I had never ever known before! And then, after what seemed like a few minutes, the light was gone. I looked over at my husband, but he was still sound asleep. If I had to describe in words what I had experienced, I would say that it was as if the light was saying, "I am God and I am love." I lay in bed for a long time, thinking about what had just happened, until I finally fell asleep.

The next morning, I didn't know what to think. I knew what had happened the night before, and I was convinced it was real, but I didn't know what to do about it. It was very confusing when I tried to understand it. Why did God's light flow into me? I'm just an ordinary, average, run-of-the-mill person, a woman with a husband, three nearly-grown kids, and two dogs. I have always tried to live by the teachings of Christ and the church, but I'm no saint. I have plenty of weaknesses and shortcomings.

I knew if I told anyone about the light, they would think I was crazy, so I kept it to myself for a year and a half. I did start attending church regularly at the Ellsworth United Methodist Church. It helped just to be with a group of people who believe in God. But that wasn't enough. Somehow I felt called to do more, so I started praying and meditating every morning. It felt like something I had to do. But despite these things I became more and more depressed. I had all these new feelings and thoughts and beliefs that I'd never had before and I was in turmoil. Finally, at my request, my pastor recommended a Christian counselor. That was the best thing for me. She asked me why I was there and I told her that I had the overwhelming feeling that I had to serve God, and that it was a totally new feeling for me. I didn't know how to serve God, I didn't know how other people served God, and I didn't know who to talk to about it. She looked surprised and asked why I felt this way. I was very apprehensive to tell her about the light, but I did and she was so very accepting of my story. She helped me feel like I wasn't crazy, and that the light really happened and it was okay to talk about it to people I felt I could trust.

When the light came, it was as if somehow a computer chip of new ideas, thoughts, and beliefs was also implanted in me at the same time that my heart was filled with love. For example, I had totally new feelings about death and dying. Cemeteries used to make me very, very uncomfortable, but now when I drive by them I have this feeling that all the people there are at peace.

Another change is that I no longer fear death! I don't know why. I just know that, after death, we will be at peace, we will be with God, and all will be right. I can't explain why know this, I just have an unshakable belief that this is so. What surprises me most about this is that not being afraid of death makes me not afraid to live. I feel like I can do what I want to and not be afraid. If I die tomorrow, somehow that's okay with me now. In comparison, I used to worry much more about everyday things: the kids, driving, the dangers of life in general. But somehow, life doesn't seem so dangerous anymore and not nearly as scary. God is in control of my life and all is right with my world!

Sometimes I feel guilty, feeling this much at peace, but then I remind myself that I didn't ask for the light to come and I wasn't praying for any kind of change in my life. It just happened to me and only God knows why. I can only assume he has something in mind for me to do. I don't know what, yet, but if I follow my heart and listen to God, I pray that I will be shown what God's plan is for my life.

When The Spirit Of Truth Comes

Elaine Scrivens

"When the Spirit of truth comes, he will guide you into all the truth; for he will not speak on his own, but will speak whatever he hears, and he will declare to you the things that are to come." (v. 13)

I am a wife and mother of three boys. Ten years ago, when the boys were nine, six, and three, I went on a parish retreat. At that time I knew that God wanted me to do something, but I kept pretending I didn't know what. I was too frightened to let him take control. I had just returned to full-time teaching and saw that as my vocation. My sons were young, and I was already very involved with my local church.

While on the retreat, someone spoke to us about the willingness of a young Jewish girl to accept the will of God without question. After the talk we had a period of silence, and I decided to go for a walk to reflect on what I had heard. The retreat house was in a beautiful countryside setting, and as I walked I wept and finally fell to my knees and promised God that, although I still wasn't sure what he wanted me to do, whatever it was, I would do it.

I felt so full of joy, I actually sat on the ground and laughed and cried. If anyone had seen me, they would have thought me mad!

I returned to the retreat house, and as I opened the door there was a gust of wind and a leaflet flew off the table and onto the floor. Thinking nothing of it, I picked up the leaflet and nearly died. It was for a local ordination course, run on a part-time basis. My initial reaction was, "You've got to be kidding!"

Two hours later, I went for a talk with my vicar, who had helped organize the weekend. I told him of my walk in the woods, and his words were something like, "Great, now I can put you forward for ordination." I was amazed, as he had never hinted about anything like this before. To be honest, I still didn't believe it, but over the next six months I received so much confirmation from other people, including my dear husband and sons, that this is what I should do, that eventually I agreed to be put forward for selection. I was selected and I'm now in my third year of ministry.

A Prayer For Help

Give ear to my words, O Lord; give heed to my sighing. (v. 1)

Patricia C. Joyce

On May 3, 2002, I was engaged to narrate the historical Williamsburg tour. At about 10:20 a.m., a few minutes before we began the walking tour, a small red car darted in front of our bus, causing the driver to hit his brakes hard and swerve to the right. I was standing, facing the passengers and narrating while holding onto the support rail. The force of the bus's braking and swerving spun me around and I became airborne, bouncing off the driver's right arm and hitting the dashboard twice. My final fall left me lying on the landing beside the driver, my shoeless right foot pointing up the steps to the center aisle and my left foot pointing toward the bus door. My eyeglasses had flown off and I was left disoriented and bewildered.

As I regained consciousness, my immediate prayer was, "Oh, Lord, please don't let anything happen to me. You know I have to get home to Mom." At that moment a feeling of peace swept through my terrified soul and I knew everything would be okay. What a revelation. What peace.

Thoughtful passengers rushed to assist me, but I said, "No, please don't move me. Let me see if anything is broken." I began wiggling my ankles and toes, bending my wrists, and moving my fingers. I moved my head in all directions and moved my torso back and forth. I found no apparent broken bones and felt no immediate pain. We went on with the tour, which ended with the bus' return to the hotel at 5:00 p.m. I immediately left to feed my 94-year-old mother, in the nursing home with contracted osteoarthritis. Afterward, at 7:30 p.m., I went to Urgent Care for x-rays and an MRI, which indicated no broken bones — *a miracle* — although they did indicate a disc misalignment that requires medication and monthly doctor visits. But I felt this was *another miracle*! No broken hip! The bus driver said he was surprised my back wasn't broken. The Lord heard my prayer and I was able to attend to Mom, who has been a nursing home resident for almost fifteen years. She gave me the best years of her life and it is my Christian ministry to support her and return the love and caring that I received.

I give thanks throughout each day for the many blessings I have been granted.

Jackie Scully

It was 1997, and my husband, two children, and I were preparing for a big move from Wisconsin to Connecticut. I planned a house-hunting weekend with my son, who was seven at the time. My husband couldn't get away, so he and our daughter stayed back. We flew into LaGuardia on a late flight (less expensive) that landed at about 10:30. After we got our bags, we shuttled to the Hertz rental car building to pick up our car so we could make the drive to New Haven. When they ran my credit card, it was rejected. I had purposely called the credit union the day we left to be sure I had plenty of credit and they assured me it was fine. Well, it wasn't fine. The card was rejected, they wouldn't take a personal check, and they were closing in fifteen minutes at midnight.

I was trying to act like I was calm and collected, but I was far from it. It was two minutes to midnight and the man behind the counter said we had to leave so they could lock the door. He was completely unconcerned that I was a woman with a seven-year-old child and nowhere to go at midnight in New York City.

I walked over to the corner of the room and implored God, "I have no options left and I can't spend the night outside with my son. Help me now." We had started walking toward the door when it opened for a pleasant-looking Indian man with a briefcase. "Can anyone direct me to New Haven?"

He drove us to New Haven and bought McDonald's for my son, and we exchanged phone numbers and addresses. I called him a week later to thank him again, but got a recording that the number was not in service. I had a feeling that would be the case.

Stranger On A Fence Post

Bonnie Compton Hanson

Suddenly an angel touched him and said to him,
"Get up and eat." (v. 5b)

Pulling his coat tight against the bitter wind, the old man stopped at the crest of Blue Bank Hill, near Flemingsburg, Kentucky. Above him, the winter sky pinked with the first blush of dawn: a blush reflected in the snow all around him and in the treacherous ice beneath his feet.

Just in front of him, the road dropped off like a roller coaster — a roller coaster coated with deadly ice! Beside him, his weary mules chomped at their bits, their warm breath forming instant puffs in the freezing air. Behind them loomed the wagonload of railroad ties they had been pulling ever since four o'clock that morning along twisting, unpaved eastern Kentucky mountain roads. They were ties that he himself had logged and dressed from his own forest, for although he was already 75, Reason ("Reece") Hinton was still as strong and ramrod-straight as a man half his age.

But was he strong enough to make it down that hill without losing his load, his mules, or even his own life? If only he had known about this ice when he left home! Then he could have asked one of his sons or grandsons to come along — though they probably would have had the sense not to in such weather. Unfortunately, Reece Hinton was a stubborn man, to his usual regret. But, somehow, God always managed to come through to help him out of all of his difficulties.

For instance, when he was very small, his beloved mother, Clarinda, had died. But God brought a new mother into his life, whom he came to love just as deeply. Then, after he was grown and married, and the children came one after another — eight in all — his wife, Laura Belle, was always in poor health. Then he, himself,

147

became so ill that the doctor feared for his life. "Dear God," he had prayed then, "please let me live long enough to raise all of these little ones. If you do, I will serve you with my whole life."

God answered that prayer beyond all expectation. Indeed, Reece hadn't been sick a day since. In gratitude, he vowed to spend his life learning the scriptures and praising God. Eventually, he committed whole chapters of the Bible to memory. Also, he used the beautiful voice God had given him to sing God's praises everywhere he went, including hymns he composed himself.

Even as he stood in his current predicament, "O God Our Help In Ages Past" burst into his mind, begging to be sung. But he needed every ounce of energy possible to keep his wagon from careening out of control on the way down that hill. Not enough brake action could cause a wild, and possibly deadly, plunge; too much could lock the wheels, jerking them sideways and pitching those heavy logs forward onto his helpless mules.

Still praying, he spoke encouragingly to the protesting animals, then clicked the reins. As they lunged, he jerked the wooden brake stick back and forth to maintain control. Inch by inch, they moved forward. Then, suddenly, the wagon began gaining momentum while the mules fought in vain for footing on the glass-slick ice.

Desperate, now, Reece fought with the brake, his fingers almost frozen from the cold and the effort. But between the ice and the down slope, and with the rapidly increasing speed, he was quickly losing the battle.

"Dear God!" he prayed out loud, "If you're going to help me, please do it *quick!*"

"Hey there, Mister, could you-all use an extra hand?"

Jerking around, Reece saw a farmer sitting on a fence post beside the road. Not even stopping to wonder why anyone would be out there this bitterly cold morning, Reece yelled back, "Sure could, son."

In a moment the stranger had reached him. "Can't blame you. This hill is almost impossible when it's iced up like this. Headed into town?"

"Right. Got to deliver this load of ties. Sure glad to see a friendly face."

Reece expected the man to help with the reins up front, or to pull back on the wagon from behind. Instead, the stranger just put his hand on the wagon's side and walked companionably alongside it in the snow. But something remarkable happened. Instantly the mules stopped sliding; the wagon stopped skidding. They could have been traveling on flat ground!

The two men continued talking about mules and lumber and things of the Lord all the way down the hill. At the bottom, the stranger said, "Well, I guess I'd better go now."

The old man reached for his new friend's hand. "You'll never know how much I've appreciated your help, son. You-all from around here? Sorry, I didn't get your name. You know how us old men forget to...." He stopped. There was no one there. Now that all the danger was past, the stranger had simply vanished into thin air.

As soon as he returned home to his farm in Muses Mills late that night, Reece told his daughter, Alice, and his granddaughter, Ruby, about this wonderful stranger. And he continued to talk about him until his death at eighty, insisting that God had sent a Heavenly Being to help him that bitter, icy morning.

My great-grandpa never stopped thanking God for it, either!

An Offer Of Comfort

*I cry aloud to God, aloud to God, that he may hear
me. In the day of my trouble I seek the Lord; in the
night my hand is stretched out without wearying;
my soul refused to be comforted.* (vv. 1-2)

Lori Hetzel

Not more than two months after my mother passed away, and I
had my vision, I went to the grave of my ex-sister-in-law. She had
died, very suddenly, eight months before my mother died. My nieces
were having great difficulty understanding why God had taken her.
She had only been 51 years of age. One niece, in particular, had
lost all of the faith she thought she ever had. When I went to the
grave, I sat down and talked to my sister-in-law about the vision I
was blessed with after my mother had died. I asked her to help her
daughters and her son cope with the loss. I prayed that my niece's
faith would be restored, so she, too, might have a vision. It was a
damp, misty Friday afternoon. When I got back into the van to
start it up, I was overcome by a very strong scent of flowers. Carnations came to my mind. I stopped the van and looked out the
windows to see if there were any flowers there that I might have
been smelling. I rolled down the window to get a better view, but
there were no flowers. I rolled up the window and just kept breathing deeply. It was if I had just walked into a floral shop, the smell
was so strong. It lasted for a minute or two. I called my husband
Karl on my cell phone to tell him where I was, and to tell him
about what had just happened. I had a feeling he, too, was wondering about my senses!

I was completely overcome by yet another experience from
our Lord. I phoned my niece when I got home, a little hesitantly I
might add, to ask her what her mother's favorite flower had been.

She told me it was carnations. I told her about the visit I had with her mom. She was a bit angry that I was having all these things happen. "Why can't I?" she said, crying. I told her, "Before the Lord will open your eyes, you must believe in him. Find your faith. There is a Heaven. She is there. Open your heart and your eyes, and all will be revealed." I continue to talk to her, and try to help her find her love of God. I pray that those who are lost, who are grieving, will look to our Lord and let him reveal the great power he has to heal the hearts that are heavy.

Healing

O Lord my God, I cried to you for help, and you have healed me. O Lord, you brought up my soul from Sheol, restored me to life from among those gone down to the Pit. (vv. 2-3)

Robert Murdock

In the fall of 1999, I went into the hospital, supposedly for just a couple of days, only to find out that I had a much more serious problem than I had realized.

I prayed for help. The help came in a different form than I expected. I was told I needed open-heart surgery, which I really didn't want to have at that time. I was physically run-down and mentally mixed up. The surgeon preferred that my mind be clear before surgery. I knew that I had to go home for that, although the doctors did not advise it.

The morning I was to go home, I woke to a sunny day. However, all I could see was fog and haze. I couldn't hear, either. But this fog cleared up my confusion. The Lord came to me in the fog and made me see that I had to have the surgery, but first I had to go home. The Lord made up my mind for me.

Even though the doctors were reluctant to release me, they let me go because I was so determined. I was at home for two weeks and never had a single worry about the surgery. Being at home made me realize that I was in the Lord's hands.

Two weeks later, on a Tuesday morning, when I returned to the hospital for the surgery, I felt no fear. I knew I was in God's hands. At some point between the time of the surgery and when I woke the next morning, I had the most beautiful vision. I was in a very bright place, so brilliant that I can't describe it in words. I was looking down upon my family. They were gathered all around me, and I beamed at them with joy. We were all together. It was perfect. I felt as if I were floating on a cloud. The words of a song came to me, "He touched me and made me whole."

Wednesday, when I awoke, I had only chest tubes and a catheter remaining from the surgery. I felt I had been healed. I had no pain and I never took pain medication. I was up and walking the same day. The next day, all of the tubes were removed and I was moved out of ICU. The nurses were amazed. They sensed my healing had been extraordinary. Before my surgery, they didn't think I would be out of the hospital until Christmas. As is turned out, I returned home the day before Thanksgiving.

Since this experience, my faith means so much more to me. Death is nothing to fear. I wonder why I was so scared of the surgery before. Every day it is important for me to read the Bible and pray. The life we live today and eternal life are completely linked. No one can tell me, after this vision, that there is no eternal life. Not a day goes by that I don't think about it. The memory of that vision comes back every day.

Barbara Frank

Six years ago, I was diagnosed with nerve damage in my left arm. After two surgeries, I developed a complication called RSD (Reflex Sympathetic Dystrophy). The pain is intense and is very difficult to treat. After a year and a half of therapy, nerve blocks, six weeks at a pain clinic, and pills, pills, and more pills, I finally started feeling like my old self again. I continued exercising over the years.

In November of 2001, the condition returned again, with the addition of shoulder and neck pain. All of the original treatments started again. The pills were causing havoc in my everyday life without decreasing the pain level. Chronic pain affects the physical as well as the mental and spiritual well being. In desperate need of pain relief, I did not always question the medications I was given, there were so many.

153

When I was taken off one medication in April, I went through the nightmare of drug withdrawal. I checked on another medication and found it was another controlled substance: morphine. I immediately stopped taking that medication and went through withdrawal for a second time in two weeks. Never again!

I continued my exercise therapy and slowly tapered off the medications. The pain was slightly improved, but continued. It was difficult getting through each day. During this time, I never asked God for help, thinking there were more important things to pray for. God had always gotten me through the difficult times, so I knew this was just another bump in the road.

The pain continued. Then along came Miracle Sunday.

I found an announcement in the Sunday church bulletin asking for personal prayer requests. Of course, the first thing that came to mind was a new baby for my son and his wife to adopt. Since there was time to spare, and I was having a very bad arm day, I asked God for some pain relief. I put the prayer request aside in my mind.

On the Tuesday after Miracle Sunday, I awoke with all shoulder, neck, and arm pain gone. I thought maybe it was just a good day. Another good day followed: a good week. Now twelve not-just-good-but-*wonderful* months have gone by pain and drug free. Could this be the miracle I prayed for? Maybe my pain has not gone forever, but I thank God for the joy that he has given back to each new day.

Elaine Klemm Grau

Last January, my husband Wally began to cough. He went to the doctor several times, but became increasingly ill, until, in March, he was in severe pulmonary distress and had to be hospitalized immediately. His lungs were totally filled with scar tissue and he was put on oxygen and steroids. We didn't think he was going to make it.

One night, as I lie in bed praying the Rosary for him, the fragrance of roses filled the room. This continued to happen for three nights while I was in prayer. I knew then that my prayers had been answered. I had asked Mary, and the healers, Brother Andre and Solanus Casey, to pray for him. The next day, for the first time, the doctor told us that he was showing improvement and would recover. Today, Wally has no residual scar tissue in his lungs.

In the Body of Christ, those on the "other side" will always pray for us when we ask. It has strengthened my faith, knowing that not only will people here pray for us, but also that those in the Communion of Saints will ask God for his healing grace. And how wonderful it is that sometimes we receive a sign that our prayers have been answered!

The Silver Wolf

Susan D. Jamison

*He has rescued us from the power of darkness and
transferred us into the kingdom of his beloved Son,
in whom we have redemption, the forgiveness of
sins.* (vv. 13-14)

It was June 16, 1998. I was in a therapy session, using visualization to work through issues from my recent divorce. I felt as if
I would never be free from my ex-husband's anger and the verbal
attacks that occurred each time we talked. My emotional buttons
were continually being pushed and I didn't like my own reactions.

In addition to therapy, I do Shamanic Journeying, which is
historically a Native/Aboriginal spiritual practice. The classic text
explaining it is *The Way of the Shaman*, by Michael Harner. Early
on in the practice of Shamanic Journeying, one receives a power
animal that acts as a guide and teacher. Mine is a silver wolf, and
I believe that Silver Wolf (as I affectionately call him) came to be
my power animal because the figure of a silver wolf represents
God in Martin Bell's writings, which I have read and used in
preaching.

During my therapy session, I was visualizing standing and facing my ex-husband and imagining what was still binding us together. My therapist told me to take all the time I needed to cut
loose whatever it was that bound us together. The image I had was
of layers and layers of barbed wire that encircled us from shoulders to ankles. When I struggled to break free I couldn't because
my hands were not free and each movement made the wire cut into
my skin. So, I mentally asked for help. In my visualization, Silver
Wolf came and began chewing through the barbed wire, layer by
layer, beginning at my shoulders and working down toward my
feet. When my arms were free I was able to take wire cutters and

remove the rest of the wire myself. Once I began to participate in the process of freeing myself, Silver Wolf stood aside and allowed me to finish, which was very empowering. After I was free I turned to thank him and saw that he was bleeding from the cuts he received in the process of helping to set me free. I felt badly that he had been injured, but I somehow knew that he had done it voluntarily, out of love for me. He wanted me to be free from this bondage. Then I realized that this was the meaning of Christ's being wounded for my sake, that Jesus willingly chose to suffer pain so that I might be set free and made whole. As I thanked him, Silver Wolf began to lick my wounds to help them heal. Such a tender and gentle love was overwhelming. I sobbed for a long time as it washed over me. Finally I was able to tell my therapist what I had experienced.

I continue to do Shamanic Journeying as part of my spiritual practice, and ever since that day, on those occasions when Silver Wolf appears, he has scars on his mouth from where he was cut by the barbed wire that he chewed for me. It is a constant reminder of the tremendous love God has for me. This does not fit any "orthodox" teaching about the meaning of the crucifixion, but it has helped me understand that particular part of Jesus' story, a part I have always struggled with because I never could accept the orthodox interpretations. My understanding of the crucifixion does not focus on Jesus saving me from my sin so that I might reach heaven after death, but focuses on God setting me free from all that binds me so that I might have a life full of abundance here and now.

I am happy to report that my relationship with my former husband is no longer hostile. We share custody of our children, he has remarried, and I am grateful every day for the opportunities I have to reflect that love to others.

157

The Presence Of Angels

The Lord appeared to Abraham by the oaks of
Mamre, as he sat at the entrance of his tent in the
heat of the day. He looked up and saw three men
standing near him. When he saw them, he ran from
the tent entrance to meet them, and bowed down
to the ground. (vv. 1-2)

Jeanne Jones

Several years ago, before we moved to Wisconsin, I was an honorary nanny for our pastor's son, Jonathan. I took care of him from the time he was able to walk until our pastor moved, when Jonathan was about five. We had wonderful times together. One time, when I was at their house, and we had been doing some spiritual direction together, Pastor Michael asked me if I knew the name of my guardian angel. He said that his was named "Susan." I guess it hadn't occurred to me that guardian angels had names, but when I backed the car out of the driveway, I said to no one in particular (or to my angel if he/she was listening), "I don't know what your name is, but I think I'll call you Jonathan." I heard a voice in my head say, "You may call me that if you wish, but my name is Michael." And then I saw my angel. He was like no angel I had ever imagined, because he was large, wide, and dressed in what I would call Viking clothes. He didn't have wings. He reminded me of some of the characters in a *B.C.* comic strip. But there was no question that he was, and is, a powerful protector.

Andrea Woodard

I have always believed in angels, ever since I can remember. I thought of angels, as many do, with glowing halos over their heads, white gowns, and clear-as-crystal wings.

That image changed last year. It was my sophomore year in college at the University of Wisconsin-Whitewater. I was attending my weekly Campus Crusade for Christ worship meeting. It was exactly one week after September 11, and my spirit was kind of down. At our meeting, we always close with some songs. I normally sing, but I just didn't feel in the mood, and it was a song I didn't know well. As I was looking around at everyone else praising through song, my attention was drawn up to the ceiling. I'm not exactly sure why I looked up, but I'm glad I did. Nothing could have prepared me for what my eyes saw. On top of a hanging light fixture, at the front of the room, I saw a greenish-yellow, glowing light. I thought my eyes were playing tricks on me, so I glanced down at the floor for a second and shook my head, then looked up again. I focused on the light fixture a little harder, trying to make out exactly what it was that I was seeing up there. Sure enough, the greenish-yellow glowing light was still shining brightly.

This was not my imagination! Slowly, I made out a silhouette of shoulders and a head, and soon the figure lifted up its hands to the heavens, like some people do when they are singing God's hymns or worshiping. I was so shocked that I didn't even think to tap my friend, Laura, who was standing next to me. My body just froze up in amazement.

After I had been looking at the angel for about ten seconds, another one appeared next to it, sitting on the light, but this one didn't have its hands lifted up like the other one. I could just make out the silhouette of its shoulders and head. It was outlined by the glowing light, exactly like the first one.

I will never forget those angels, and I feel blessed to have witnessed such an amazing sight. I know that many people will never get to see such a thing in their lifetimes. God is alive and active in our world. His angels have protected me numerous times, especially last year when I was in a bus that slid off the road and almost flipped over while doing a 360-degree spin. Now every time I go to Crusades, I look up when I'm singing, hoping that the angels will visit me again.

E. Von Bruck

Upon my college graduation, I was employed as a foreign language teacher in a Christian liberal arts college in Barrington, Rhode Island. I seemed to spend more time counseling students than correcting their homework and tests. Soon I realized that I was more concerned about people's hearts than about their education, although I had ability to tend to both.

After two years of teaching there, I had the great privilege of hearing about Francis Schaeffer, who later became a well-known Christian author and philosopher. I decided to embark on another journey into the unknown. I resigned from teaching to study under this man's inspiration. His brilliant intellect, coupled with great compassion and Christian faith (sic) sparked a new fire in my heart. He and his family lived high up in the Swiss Alps, overlooking magnificent glistening glaciers and deep, lush, green valleys. Some farmers would take their cows up the mountains to graze, and their cowbells resounded like an orchestra in joyful celebration.

It was there at L'Abri, as the Schaeffer's home was called, that I asked God to anoint my piano playing with his music and song. It was there that I began to compose sacred music in glory to his name. It was there that I met the love of my life, a missionary's son who later was killed in a car crash. It was there that God surrounded me with his presence again and renewed my love for him and my desire to serve him

One winter's night, upon receiving some disturbing news, I ran up the hills through woods and fields to find a place to cry and pray. I found a shack filled with hay and, with my face buried in my hands, I cried to the Lord. Soon I was comforted and immersed in an inexplainable (sic) peace. I simply basked in this wonderful, calming balm without realizing night had fallen. I covered myself with hay in the hopes of surviving the night there, but the air became unbearably cold. Finally, I headed out into the darkness. Shivering, I went faster and faster through the thick black forest. When I arrived at the edge of the woods and saw the village lights, I wondered how on earth I managed to come down this dark mountain so quickly without fear or falling. I turned around to view the path of my descent. To my astonishment, I saw the path behind me all lit up and lined with hovering angels.

By then it was 2 or 3 a.m. When I saw a light still burning in the Schaeffer's guest study, I knocked, and my beloved opened the door saying, "My dear, your face is lit up like an angel." I simply nodded and told no one what had occurred.

Edeltraud Von Bruck, *Voyage: The Journey to Eternal Glory* (Lake Mary: Creation House Press, 2000), pp. 19-20.

Steadfast Love

Steadfast love and faithfulness will meet; righteousness and peace will kiss each other. Faithfulness will spring up from the ground, and righteousness will look down from the sky. (vv. 10-11)

Christal Bindrich

My brother died on March 15, 2001, at the age of 56. We were very close and each of us always knew when something was wrong with the other. His death was a very difficult adjustment for me.

I felt his presence, his spirit, was still with me. He had a great sense of humor and was the one who always lightened the grief in the family at a relative's passing by recalling funny stories. He had a firm belief in the eternal life that is promised us by the death and resurrection of Jesus Christ. He faced his death bravely and without fear.

Several months after his death, he visited me in a dream. In this dream, someone was trying to wake me. I am very difficult to wake up in the morning. I felt like water was being thrown in my face and I could feel someone reaching down and giving me a kiss on the cheek. I screamed in my dream and said, "Okay, I'm awake! You didn't need to throw water on me!"

When I opened my eyes, no one was there. My face was dry, except for the kiss on my cheek. I knew my brother had come one more time to say the good-bye we didn't get to say at the time of his death. He came to tell me it was all going to be all right.

Vickie Eckoldt

Having the greatest grandparents anyone could ever have was a real blessing for me. So, when my grandparents died, it left a big void in my life. Grandpa passed away first. A week after his funeral, I was asleep one night when I heard his voice call my name. Then he appeared for a brief moment, with that beautiful smile on his face, and said to me, "I'm fine, I'm happy now, so please don't cry for me anymore."

Two years later, a similar event occurred after Grandma's passing. She appeared wearing the blue dress she was laid out in, and she said, "I am happy now that I am with Grandpa. We are fine, so stop shedding so many tears. I will always watch over you." And then she was gone, but I have felt her presence many times when I needed her.

I was 25 years old when my father passed away after a six-month battle with lung cancer. Mother could not accept that her husband was dying at the age of 52. She left it to me to make all of the funeral arrangements.

One night, not long after the service, a foggy, white haze hung over my bed. Inside the haze I saw a vision of my father. He was healthy again. I watched as he looked around his grave at the cemetery. His eyes met mine and he whispered the words, "You did a good job." Then he smiled at me and was gone. I will always cherish this beautiful gift.

The Taste Of Music

Jeanne Jones

*So if you have been raised with Christ, seek the
things that are above, where Christ is, seated at
the right hand of God. Set your minds on things
that are above, not on things that are on earth, for
you have died, and your life is hidden with Christ
in God.* (vv. 1-3)

The whole thing began when I was asked to be the song leader
for a Walk to Emmaus retreat in 1988. I was a kindergarten teacher
and sang in the choir, but no one had ever asked me to lead singing
for adults, and I was amazed at having been chosen. I felt comfortable with the task. It didn't require a really good voice, as the singing was mostly used to gather people together after break time and
as a time-filler if needed. I had a back-up guitarist who had a good
voice, and I knew the leadership team could all sing, so I attended
the training sessions and felt really happy and excited about the
weekend. But when I arrived in Phoenix, I got sick. I had a stom-
achache, and it wouldn't go away. I ate Tums, I ate crackers, I
sipped water ... I felt lousy. If I had been stressed, I could have
blamed that, but I knew I wasn't stressed. At times I felt that there
were two of me, one going through the motions of enthusiastically
leading the singing, and the other watching me and wondering what
I was doing since I was so sick. The retreat started Thursday night.
By Saturday, I decided that if I wasn't better by Sunday, I would go
to the hospital and see if I had an ulcer, instead of starting for home,
100 miles away.

Saturday night we had a Healing Service and I asked for forgiveness. The thought popped into my head that I needed to forgive my mother for not loving me. This was strange, because intel-
lectually, I suppose I knew that my mother really did love me in

her own way, although she was not demonstrative. Apparently I carried those feelings inside and needed to let go of them, because the minute I said that I needed to forgive her, I was healed.

I know that God was working in my life that weekend. I think I could say that I had an "infilling" of the Holy Spirit, although I didn't know what that phrase meant before that time. I do know that when we were ready to leave, those who were the participants in the Walk were asked to stand up at the last gathering and tell what the weekend had meant to them and what they were going to do about it. Though the leaders were not expected to say anything, I got up and said that my life had changed. Not only was my pastor there, my husband and eighteen members of my home church were, too. Most were en route to Mexico for a mission trip. My husband could see such a change in me that he wondered if I was okay to go home while he went to Mexico. I was. I had Jesus with me.

For several months afterwards, every time I closed my eyes, Jesus, with his arms outstretched, was imprinted on the inside of my eyelids. I also experienced great joy and odd sensations, such as being able to taste music. I could suddenly "play by ear" instead of just reading music. It was as though the barrier between the left side and the right side of my brain was broken down and the two sides were integrated somehow. I went from being a very organized left-brained person to being a person who couldn't remember what day it was! Fortunately, that didn't last for too long, and I feel a greater sense of wholeness now than was ever possible before. Another joy was that the scriptures were "opened" to me, so that what I read earlier as words became full of life and meaning. I truly love to read the scripture now and feel God's presence in new ways each time.

As I said, it was a strange weekend. After a year of Spiritual Direction, I felt that I was to leave teaching and go into ordained ministry. God had indeed blessed me in many ways.

Assurance

*Let your steadfast love, O Lord, be upon us, even
as we hope in you.* (v. 22)

Marie Regine Redig, S.S.N.D.

Always I have been guided gently by God in how and where I
would be in ministry and career. I learned to trust God's guidance
and movement in my life. In 1987, I took the position of coordinator of the spiritual growth programs for the Ewens Center at Mount
Mary College in Milwaukee. The ministry of working with women
in the various aspects of their spiritual lives was one dear to my
heart. My life was enriched right along with theirs while I spent
fifteen years listening, counseling, and providing informational,
inspirational, and experiential classes for them. As I grew older
and realized that semi-retirement was probably in my near future,
I knew that I would leave Mount Mary and keep helping only my
private clientele out of my home office.

But when? The question often came to my mind, and I firmly
believed that God would again be present and direct me when the
time was right.

Never did I expect it to happen as it did. In January of 2002, I
went with some faculty and students on a four-day solitude retreat
at Baileys Harbor, Wisconsin. Coming away from there, I felt deeply
content and full of inspiration for starting the second semester. One
week later, on Thursday, January 24, I awoke about ten minutes
earlier than usual and lay quietly in my bed, offering my day to
God. It happened then! As clear as could be, I heard in my mind
and heart, "Gina, it's time to leave Mount Mary." I couldn't believe
it and thought it must be some figment of my imagination. I arose,
did my morning exercises, showered, and prayed. I thought the
idea would leave. It didn't! The gentle, but direct message stayed

in my face for the next four days. Finally, I confided in my two companion SSND sisters living with me. They said, "Sounds like you need to look at that."

I prayed over it and started the process for termination. As I did my work and met with people, I found myself relishing my experience and saying, "Do I really want to part with this?" Gradually, I could say, "With God's grace, I think I can let go." I left Mount Mary on June 7 with much peace in my heart, knowing that, once again, God had moved me gently and firmly. If not, I would probably still be at Mount Mary, not knowing when to stop. Yes, I trust God's messages for my future even when they come in strange ways.

Janet Beltman

The afternoon of the third Sunday in January, 1977, was a cloudy, dreary day, but it is a day I will never forget. It had been two years since my father's death, a time during which I had often felt sad and alone. Having just returned from church, I began preparing my dinner.

I was standing at the stove, with my back to the window, enveloped in the gloom of the day and my loneliness, when I became aware of a brightness in the kitchen. My first thought was that the sun had finally broken through the clouds. I turned to look outside. The dreariness had not changed, but the brightness continued to increase inside my kitchen until the entire room was filled with a brilliant yellow light. A warm, tingling sensation then began penetrating the top of my head and slowly traveled down through my body. As it exited through my fingertips and toes, the brightness in the room began to fade away. When the sensation completely left my body, the room had returned to its former dreariness.

I felt frightened at first. What had just happened to me? But then I remembered the warmth and comfort that had flowed through me with the light, and I realized that God had sent the Holy Spirit to assure me, in the midst of my gloom, that I am never alone.

God's peace and presence is a blessing. God is good.

Lorina

Steve Taylor

Restore us, O Lord God of hosts; let your face shine, that we may be saved. (v. 19)

Her name was Lorina. She was only 22 years old, yet, somehow she seemed to be carrying far too much sorrow for someone who had seen so few years. I met her at a Bible study held at Gary and Rosa's home. He, one of our pastors, and she, an ordained minister as well, had begun a Bible study for young adults. And in our military community, on another continent far from home, there were certainly hundreds of young, single adults. Though I was almost forty years old, my wife had recently returned to the United States, and, at least for the moment, I qualified as being "temporarily single." So, Rosa had invited me, probably more out of sympathy and a desire to keep me out of trouble than out of any sense that I might somehow be helpful in this endeavor.

The Bible study was not much different than many Bible studies that I have attended. Rosa did a good job with the book of Numbers, and it was interesting and enlightening, but the real reason for being there was not evident until after the evening study was complete. At that time, we joined together in a circle and we began to pray, each person as they felt led. As these young people prayed, I began to understand why many of them were here. Their prayers were filled with cries to God to enter into their lives and take away their pain: emotional and spiritual pain that had cut deep into their beings. The pain of being alone and afraid. The pain of being disconnected from family and community and home.

After we closed the prayer, I noticed that many of the younger folks gravitated toward some of us older folks. They began to talk. They spoke of their joys and their pains. They spoke of the loneliness of being away from home, and they talked about their hopes for the future. Lorina was sitting next to me and we entered into small talk — the kind you make when you are not quite sure what to say — until I asked her about her dreams for her future. Then, ever so softly, she began to cry. Through the tears and the silent sobs, she told me she had no dreams. She spoke of a tragic past that had swept away her dreams. She spoke about the death of her mother and the sexual abuse from her father. She talked about how she was often afraid, and that she had considered suicide — for certainly, death could not be any worse than the emotional hell in which she lived.

I must admit, I felt almost overwhelmed by the horror and intensity of her story. Yet as she talked, the Holy Spirit began to work and a very strange idea began to grow. I thought, "I know, I will ask her to come to visit a refugee camp." And after I verbalized this idea, she sat and stared deeply into my eyes for a long time. I almost felt as if I could reach right down into her and touch her soul. It was a very real moment, one of those times when you know that something profound is happening. Slowly she nodded her head yes.

The next Saturday, she was there at our appointed meeting place. I was a bit surprised that she had joined us. I honestly had not expected her to show. During the ride to the camp, another friend and I talked about how we would often see God at work in the camps, even in the midst of so much suffering. We admitted that, though it might seem strange, the light of God would shine there in ways that it would never shine back in the relative comfort and safety of our daily lives.

Lorina listened, but didn't respond much.

We entered the camp and went about our various tasks of delivering food, medicine, and school supplies. I was very busy and soon lost track of Lorina. After a while, I saw her again.

There she was, sitting on a log bench, surrounded by maybe a dozen children. She was touching their faces, caressing their hair, and talking to them, giving herself to each one around her. And as I looked into her face, it was absolutely radiant. I was so shocked that I almost staggered. There, in the person of this tortured young girl, was the person of Jesus, surrounded by lonely and damaged children, sharing their pain and showing his love.

During the day I saw her several more times, moving through the camp, always surrounded by dozens of children, sometimes with as many as eight or nine holding her hands.

We left the camp that day, more reflective than usual. Normally, everyone would be talkative and expressive, but this day there was an uncharacteristic silence. After awhile, I looked at Lorina and asked the question, "Well, what do you think?"

Often times, this question asked to folks experiencing the camp for the first time would elicit a whole host of comments, from discussing the camp conditions to discussing the theological implications for the church. Answers would almost always be punctuated with an excited mannerism. Yet, when she answered, it was with three simple words. Three simple words expressed out of heartfelt conviction and from a deeply scarred soul: three simple words on which her hope now hung, and which her life, on this day, had expressed. She quietly said, "God is good...."

God is good....

Witnesses To The Light

Kay Boone Stewart

When Jesus saw her, he called her over and said,
"Woman, you are set free from your ailment."
(v. 12)

A year and a half ago I was diagnosed with a virulent form of breast cancer. It began with an "iffy" diagnosis and quickly accelerated into something they call the "ugly tumor."

A team of doctors was conscripted, a surgery was scheduled, and a large and faithful prayer team emerged. At this point we still thought it was merely ductile carcinoma in situ: a pre-cancer, my doctor called it.

On the scheduled morning, I found myself staring at the ceiling of the operating room where a highly-skilled woman surgeon, who was also a Christian, arrived to operate. I felt very calm, knowing that God was in control. We chatted, making small talk and joking. Soon I was under the anesthetic.

Half a continent away, my sister Lynne and her daughter, Vanessa, sat down together to pray for me. They prayed, in their time zone, at a time concurrent with ours. They had only prayed a short while when a vision started coming to my sister. It was different from anything she had ever witnessed while in prayer. She could see me on the operating table with the medical staff around me, working over me. Then she observed that the entire room was crammed with beings of light. They were gathered around, watching, and occasionally one would put hands to the task along with the doctor, reaching into the surgical opening and arranging things.

"It went very smoothly," the doctor told me afterward. "I feel certain we got it all."

When I got home, my sister called and told me about the vision. I was stunned.

171

"They really roll out the angelic host for ductile carcinoma in situ," I joked, feeling very blessed indeed to have had so much help. "Imagine what they'd send for a real emergency!"

The next week I went in for my post-op appointment with the oncologist. He showed me into his office and closed the door.

"I have some bad news," he told me. "The lab report came back and the tumor removed was one we don't like to see. We call it the 'ugly one.' It likes to hide in tissue, is invasive, and frequently comes back."

Another surgery was scheduled. My surgeon cleaned up more ductile carcinoma and took a look around for more of the "bad guy."

"I was very surprised," she told me afterward. "We had to re-move three lymph nodes under your arm. It had traveled."

Now I was upset. This meant chemotherapy and radiation. Originally I had been slated for only radiation.

But through it all, I never doubted that I would survive. My trust was in my Savior. And my mind kept returning to the scene in the hospital operating room during that first surgery. What a special blessing it had been to know the help God sends when we are in peril. I'm sure the same "team" or one like it assembled the second time. But why were there so many?

Perhaps I'll never know. But many, many people prayed for me — even people I didn't know. Could it be that each person praying for me was represented there by a being of light?

Singapore Angel

Mary DeMuth

Keep your lives free from the love of money, and
be content with what you have; for he has said, "I
will never leave you or forsake you." So we can
say with confidence, "The Lord is my helper; I
will not be afraid. What can anyone do to me?"
(vv. 5-6)

"Miss, you need to step here." The woman's voice came from behind me. I was alone in Singapore, recently de-trained from Kuala Lumpur, Malaysia, where I had finished a six-week short-term mission. It had been an adventure of faith; I had gone to assist a vibrant Christian church in its youth and vocal programs in a Muslim country, and I went alone. I was 22, wide-eyed and full of zeal, but that night at the train station, I was tired and afraid. Just a week prior, my new Malaysian friends had taken me to the closest emergency room, where the doctor gave me spoiled medicine for a severe case of bronchitis. My body heaved until the medicine was out of my system, so I was still a bit green on the long train ride.

Earlier, the Lord had sent two Taiwanese men, whom I befriended on the train, to help me unload my heavy luggage onto the deserted Singapore platform. Friends greeted them after they detrained; they shyly waved to me as they laughed with their friends and sped away. A few families met the other remaining passengers, and I was left alone.

Taxis did not run after midnight, and my only connection to where I would be staying that evening was a scribbled address that I clutched in my right hand. My pastor from home had told me a harrowing tale of his handing this same address to a taxi driver and getting a grand tour of Singapore. A few taxicabs later, my pastor had finally arrived at the compound. Other mission teams that filtered through Singapore told similar stories of trying unsuccessfully to find this out-of-the-way place.

Stressed, I sat on my barely luggable luggage, put my face in my hands, and prayed, "Oh Lord, help me!" That's when the woman's voice interrupted my pity party.

"Miss, you need to step here."

I turned around to find a short Chinese woman, probably in her sixties. She was small-boned and seemed frail, but her voice exuded confidence. Before I could explain my predicament and my need for the nonexistent taxi, she motioned for me to follow her to the street to the left of the platform. Awkwardly, I dragged my two suitcases off the platform to where she now stood, beckoning.

"Follow me, Miss. Don't worry. I will take care of you." I showed her the compound's address. She smiled and told me to wait. I stood on the dark street feeling vulnerable. *Maybe this is a plot. Maybe she's going to rob me.* In minutes she returned and a taxi followed her, backing down the road toward me. Again she said, "Don't worry. I will take care of you."

Before I could get to my luggage, this woman — who probably weighed ninety pounds — grabbed my bags and effortlessly hurled them into the taxi's already open trunk. She opened the back door for me and then spoke to the taxi driver in Chinese. Her voice raised as she motioned erratically with her arms. The taxi driver nodded. She turned to me and repeated, "Don't worry. I will take care of you." With that, she shut my door and the car lurched forward. I tried to blurt out a thank you as the door slammed, but its impact absorbed my words.

Desperately wanting to thank her, I turned to look out the taxi's back window where she stood. At least I could wave and smile. But when I looked, she was gone. The street, deserted, showed no signs of any life; only the hazy yellow glow of streetlights remained. The taxi driver took me directly to the compound, via palm tree-lined streets, and took my luggage from the trunk. He waited until I found someone inside and then sped off.

Only once in my life have I possibly encountered an angel. The Bible speaks of wildly masculine angels whose strength and form cause people to quake. My "angel" was cleverly disguised as an aging Chinese woman who helped me find a taxi one quiet Singapore night.

Safe

Claire Hunston

In your book were written all the days that were
formed for me, when none of them as yet existed.
How weighty to me are your thoughts, O God! How
vast is the sum of them! I try to count them — they
are more than the sand; I come to the end — I am
still with you. (vv. 16b-18)

It was late September of 1990. My stepson, 37 years of age, was terminally ill with lung cancer, metasticized from other parts of his body that the disease had attacked first. His wife called us from their home in another city and told us the somber news. She was resigned, but ill at ease. I sensed her distress and desperately wanted to help. My husband and I prayed, then I prayed again, and again, that there might still be a turn around or, at the least, that his wife might find some peace in her agony.

I went to our library to hunt down every book I could find that talked about healing or miracles, so I might better know how to pray. I brought home four or five that I thought might help — two were by Bernie Siegel. I opened his book on miracles and read. If only some of those miraculous stories could apply to my stepson. There were plenty of reasons why he should live and not die so young. For one, we all loved him, even more so, it seemed, as he was almost passing from our reach. My heart was overwhelmed with the possibility that a miracle could happen and that he would stay among us.

Suddenly, I stopped reading, looked out beyond the patio door to the garden, and remembered how, just two weeks earlier, he had sat with us at the table and laughed gently as he shared a thought with his half-sister (our daughter) whom he had just come to know. She was sixteen and she was so proud to call him her brother. The brief visit had been a dream fulfilled. I continued to read about another miracle and I truly began to believe that it could happen to him, too.

Then it was there. My eyes were closed, but the vision was clear. He and his wife were walking through a green meadow, moving happily along, hand in hand, laughing as though without a care. Suddenly, before them appeared an abyss. He turned to her and indicated that he would have to continue while she would stay behind. In that instant, a sleeved arm from a gray shrouded figure moved toward him and gently swept him from her, back over the abyss and beyond, to disappear into a soft gray mist. She was gone, too. My heart seemed to stop. I was confused, but strangely at peace. I was greatly relieved and, somehow, comforted that he was safe. Now, what to say to her? I opened my eyes. There was no one else in the room and I had to sort out what I had just seen. Was this just a dream or was it a foretelling of what was to come? Was I to interpret it to mean that he would die and that she would be all right with it? A few days later I called her. I told her about the vision and, although she was saddened, she was deeply touched, and she was able to be comforted. Knowing that he would be safe seemed better than worrying about the moment of his death. A few days later he was gone and we traveled the long distance to be with her. We have not talked about the vision again, but we talked about him and about how he came to her at night, as if to talk, and then he'd be gone. She is now happily remarried.

For me it is a very wonderful memory from which I still gain a measure of peace.

Can Trust In God Be Restored?

Lois Rae Carlson

The Lord looks down from heaven on humankind
to see if there are any who are wise, who seek af-
ter God. (v. 2)

It was the end of my first year as a young widow on my own with two children. We'd just moved to Chicago. My parents wanted to give me some time alone, so my dad met the moving van, helped my children unpack boxes, and took them off to music camp. I was being given an incredible gift of freedom after a year of coping with the loss of my husband and learning the pace of single parenthood.

With my move over and the children in good hands, I took some friends up on an offer to use their chalet in Switzerland in the hamlet of Le Breona, near the town of La Forclas, to be alone and devote time to getting to know God better. Before long, I was on an Alpine trail hiking the two-hour trek up the mountain.

But instead of freedom, I was feeling anguish. At first I thought it was only a side effect of exhaustion from the move, the long flight from the United States, and the strenuous hike. But as I sat alone on the chalet's terrace, I saw that while I had expected to be feeling closer to God, I was actually questioning his very existence. I was consumed with bitterness about my husband's passing and with fear for my children's future — and my own. I felt stupid and naïve to have ever believed in God.

On top of feeling I'd lost touch with God, I suddenly realized that when my friend had led me to the chalet, I'd been so dazed by fatigue that I hadn't paid attention to the careful directions he gave me. And I was expected to be able to navigate the mountain on my own, going down to the village in the valley for more supplies.

As I sat there, I wasn't even sure in which direction the village was! The trail was full of hairpin curves with side paths to the other side of the mountain. I had only three days' worth of provisions. I pleaded to God for help, but I had absolutely no conviction that there was any other power at hand than my own attempt to calm my fear.

By the third day, I had only a small bit of cheese and bread left, and I knew I had to do something. As I looked out from the terrace, I noticed a flagpole several hundred yards down the mountain. A magnificent Swiss flag was flying there. I remembered passing it on the way up. I realized that using the flagpole as a marker, I could begin my journey down the mountain accurately. So I set off. But when I got to the flagpole, I felt completely stymied, not knowing whether to go right or left. Again, I prayed, but again, it felt like a futile exercise.

At that moment I heard the sound of a tractor engine, far down the mountain, but in a specific direction. I remembered that at the base of the climb there was a road paralleling the footpath for a short distance before the path turned upward. From there, it was clear to me which face of the mountain I was to stay on. Looking carefully for signs, I saw the huge pile of rocks my friend had pointed out as a landmark. I knew the sight line to the flagpole must be clear from there. Before long, excited and relieved, I found the village.

From then on, my days at the chalet were magical. Understanding now the basics of orienteering, I was all over the mountain — way beyond the tree line and down to other villages. For companionship I made friends with the marmots who were curious about my visits near their rock lair.

But despite my good humor, I still felt no peace about God. The hours of comfort and spiritual growth I'd expected from reading the Bible and Mary Baker Eddy's books were nonexistent. Instead, I found those hours frustrating and confusing; I felt no connection with the words of the books. The basic questions of my life were going unanswered. My nights were long and sleepless and troubled. I could only look forward to the freedom of my daytime hikes.

Late one afternoon I hiked farther up the mountain than ever before. The view of the vast new glacier fields across the mountain range made them bigger than the sky. The joy of exploring the earth's beauty overwhelmed me. I'd never had that kind of experience before.

Then, suddenly, I lost my footing in the loose glacier rock and slid painfully down the slope I had just climbed. I tried to get up, but my foot wouldn't support my weight. Dread set in. The bare expanse of this mountain face offered no shelter, and I knew that without extra clothing, I couldn't be safe there through the night.

The feeling of danger brought all the bitterness I'd felt about my husband's passing to the forefront. I saw my own worst fear: that I would be left alone on the earth, vulnerable and unsupported.

This time, I refused to pray. I cried again every tear of self-pity I'd ever cried before. I don't know how long I lay there in the rough gravel. The sun was setting very fast. I didn't even care what happened to me.

Then I noticed a sound. It was the small, simple sound of water — the glacier melt — trickling down the mountain. I'd noticed it before, but this time it struck me as the most beautiful sound I'd ever heard — nature's symphony. I felt the gentlest breeze on my face, cooling the heat of my tears. Then I felt, again, the stillness that for decades had characterized my faith.

"I am here," said an inner voice. "Now and always. It has always been me."

I knew this was the voice of God telling me that all the good I had ever experienced in my life, all the beauty of those innocent pleasures of my days in the Alps, had been signs of God's love for me. And I saw that my husband had never really been the source of my care and support. He was, of course, an essential proof of God's unchanging love. The forms of the love shown to me would come and go, but the love itself was constant. At that moment, I knew I could give up the disappointment in my life by understanding that the source of that love could never be altered.

Fully convinced that I was in the presence of the Divine, I stood up spontaneously. My ankle had been so swollen I couldn't remove my boot. But now it was suddenly strong and flexible.

Carefully, I maneuvered through the crushed rock and found the trail back to the chalet. I arrived just as twilight began to welcome the stars.

Many metaphors came out of my days on that mountain. The orienteering skills have reminded me, in many moments of doubt and confusion, that the Ten Commandments are reliable guides to get me off the mountains of pride and self-will. When I lose faith in God's care for me, those are almost invariably the issues — wanting something I can't have, thinking I know better than God how things ought to be, and thinking I want to do things on my own. But we can't do anything alone. Every breath, blink, and swallow show God's grace — unearned and operating in ways that nurture, support, and draw us to the origin of all the good.

Maybe that's the point — the good in our lives. In many languages, good is the name for God. How often I've overlooked the good — or belittled and dismissed it. But I'm learning to recognize the good things in life, no matter how small they may seem. And to honor the source of goodness. Even during the hardest times, we can thank God for holding us, and never believe that his absence — a vacuum — could be true.

What it all boils down to for me is that God initiates our relationship to him. He gives us the desire to know him — and the means for doing so. It's God's intention that we know how we are being loved.

Praying For A Child

Kris Drollinger

He gives the barren woman a home, making her
the joyous mother of children. Praise the Lord!
(v. 9)

My experience occurred on a Saturday morning in early November, 1988. My husband Rick and I had been trying to have a baby for about two years. We were both in our mid-thirties, so time (especially since we had hoped to have two children) was getting short. We had been going through some rather expensive fertility workups and we were in our fourth month of this effort and beginning to run low on money. I had been praying daily to the Lord at least just to give us a chance. I felt that, with God's help and guidance, Rick and I could raise a child who would make a difference — even if it were a difference in just his or her neighborhood. We felt we could raise a happy, healthy child. We had been married for ten years, so we felt we were very secure in our love for each other.

The morning in question was one of those typical early November days — frosty, some traces of unmelted snow, but not really a snow cover. My husband had gone off somewhere running simple Saturday morning errands, and I was getting set to run a few of my own in the area, walking to the mailbox and then up to a grocery store several blocks from our home. In the process of getting ready to leave, I discovered, much to my disappointment, that yet again this month I had not become pregnant. I remember standing in front of the mirror, brushing my hair and crying and praying my usual prayer to God asking for just one chance for a child.

I pulled myself together and started out to run my errands. I was standing waiting for the light to change at 92nd and Capitol Drive. The sun was shining in that weak kind of silvery way when it's trying to shine through a thin layer of clouds, and it was chilly enough that I had my jacket zipped up. The light changed, and as I stepped up onto the little island in the center of Capitol Drive, I very clearly heard a hoarse whisper, loudest in my left ear, saying, "Kris, Jesus loves you, this *you should know!*" I stepped down off the island and continued walking the rest of the way across the street, and then turned right towards the mailbox on 93rd Street. I felt shaken by the voice, but also astounded! Of course, I of all people should know how much Jesus loves me! I had the feeling like, what in the world was I thinking? From then on I absolutely knew that everything would be all right and that our prayers could most certainly be answered.

On the 29th of that same month, I went in for a fourth fertility treatment and at Christmas I was able to announce that I was, indeed, expecting a child in August 1989. Our daughter, Michelle, is now twelve years old, but the voice I heard is as clear to me today as it was on that November morning in 1988.

Call it a mother's love, but our daughter is truly a gift. She is beautiful, very involved in school, our church, and the community. She is an honor-roll student, and has been a complete joy to my husband and me as well as to the people she meets. Michelle knows this entire story, and her faith in God is very strong. I am proud to share my story with anyone who will take the time to listen because I know with every fiber of my being that this is true, not my imagination, and that a strong faith in the Lord is absolutely the only way to live, love, and be loved.

The Faith Of A Child

Jane Moschenrose

Those who love me, I will deliver; I will protect
those who know my name. When they call to me, I
will answer them; I will be with them in trouble, I
will rescue them and honor them. With long life I
will satisfy them, and show them my salvation. (vv.
14-16)

As an eleven-year-old pitcher for the Rockies Little League softball team, Karen was having a great night. The Rockies were winning, and Karen was taking an active role in her team's progress toward the championships in our mid-size midwestern community.

With the bases loaded and two outs, the pressure was on Karen. She pitched a ball outside home plate, the catcher missed it, and the player on third base started running for home. Karen ran up to cover home plate, and she caught the ball thrown by the catcher just as the runner was coming into home. As she was tapping the runner out, however, something very strange happened. The ball popped up in the air and Karen collapsed, screaming out in pain. As any mother would, I ran to her. She pointed to her right leg. I took hold of her foot and it flopped loosely, connected to her leg only by the flesh.

The EMT's were unable to splint Karen's leg or ankle, and could only support it loosely with a blanket. As we rode over the bumpy field and poorly maintained road to the hospital, Karen continued to scream out in pain. About halfway to the hospital, however, she suddenly became silent. I was sitting next to her, holding her hand, and looked at her, then at the EMT holding her leg. He seemed not to notice the change in Karen. She had an odd look on her face, her eyes weren't quite closed and seemed focused toward her left leg. For a moment I thought maybe she had died. I said,

"Karen, are you still with us?" She ever so gently squeezed my hand, and somehow I knew she was okay. She was silent the rest of the trip, and seemed oddly at peace.

After getting her settled in the emergency room, I asked her about the sudden silence. She calmly said, "Oh, Jesus came to me and told me I was going to be all right. I have five angels surrounding me."

Totally taken by surprise, I said, "You do?"

"Why, yes, can't you see them?" And she proceeded to describe where they were, surrounding her bed.

Early the next morning, as she was being prepared for surgery, Karen asked me a question. "Mama, what if the reason Jesus came to me last night was because he is going to take me home?"

Karen is our only child. I have always thought losing one's child was the worst, most intolerable thing that could happen to a parent. But somehow that morning I had no fear. Probably because God had blessed my Punkin with his presence, I was filled with an indescribable peace. I looked at Karen, right in the eyes, and said, "Punkin, don't you worry about a thing. If you see a bright light, you go for that light, because it will mean that is what's best." She seemed satisfied with that answer.

It was one thing to get through all of this and not submit to the tears that were begging release. I let them flow when we were just outside of the operating room together. Karen suddenly quoted several scripture verses. I didn't know she had any memorized! Her father calmly said, "Are those the verses you're going to take into surgery with you?" She said, "Yes," and my tears broke loose, not in fear, but in awe. I was in awe of the faith of this child, and understood in a new way what Jesus meant when the taught that we must have the faith of a child in order to see the kingdom of heaven. Karen looked up at me, saw my tears, and said, "Don't worry, Mama, the angels will take care of you."

"Are there angels here?"

"Of course, Mama! Don't you see them. There's two right there by your head!"

Naturally, Karen came through the surgery and recovery just fine.

Several months later, I asked Karen if the experience had changed her, faith-wise. I knew that my faith was much greater! She thought about it for a minute, shrugged, and said, "Oh, I don't know. I've always believed in God."

Karen had never had a serious accident or injury before, and it just made sense to her that God would come to her in her need.

"Unless you change and become like little children, you will never enter the kingdom of heaven" (Matthew 18:2).

I Am Sure That God Is Able

Linda J. Vogel

This grace was given to us in Christ Jesus before the ages began, but it has now been revealed through the appearing of our Savior Christ Jesus, who abolished death and brought life and immortality to light through the gospel. (vv. 9b-10)

In 1969 my father was dying (too slowly!) from a malignant brain tumor that changed his personality and robbed him of many life skills. He was less and less able to tell us things, because he might say he had "buttons" for breakfast when, clearly, he thought he had said "eggs." We could guess what he meant some of the time, but often there was not enough context for us to begin to guess, and he would become frustrated with us because he thought he had said what he meant. After many trips to Kansas to be with my parents, our family left for a much-needed vacation in the Northwest.

I found myself struggling with a combination of anger at God and guilt, because I felt like a hypocrite. How could I presume to teach Christian Education to others when I found my own prayers bouncing off the ceiling and felt guilty about my frustration and anger? Remember, this was before Elizabeth Kubler Ross had written her book on the five stages of grief, and no one had ever suggested to me that my feelings were "human" and that God understood!

After a lovely afternoon and early evening in the mountains in the Canadian Rockies, I settled our two youngest children, ages four and two, in the back of our VW camper. Again, this was long before parents knew that children belonged in restraining seats, and the van didn't even have seat belts, except in the front seats. My husband and our fifteen-year-old son were in the front.

All at once, our not-yet talkative two-year-old said, "Pete gone! Pete bye-bye." I turned around and then screamed with terror. The back door must not have been securely latched. When my husband had down shifted ('69 VW campers only had 53 horsepower), the door flew up and Pete must have flown out, because he was nowhere in sight!

I screamed! Dwight turned the van around, as if on a dime, and we headed back from where we had come. Around the next bend, I saw Pete, at a pull-off, in the arms of a Canadian woman. As Dwight pulled into the pull-off, I jumped out of the van.

"Mommy, you shouldn't get out of the van when it's moving. You might fall on your face!" Pete said. He had landed on his bottom and fallen back on his shoulders, but had not hit his head. There had not been a truck or car traveling behind us to hit him when he hit the pavement. Later, when Dwight and our teenaged son went back to the accident site, they found Pete's little stuffed pig, Porkchop. It had hit the guard rail and was split open where it lay down the side of the mountain. It could have been Pete.

I took my son in my arms. At that moment, that big red ball of fire that is the sun began to drop behind a mountain peak in the west. Suddenly, a great peace came over me. I knew that God gives life and God receives life in death. Death is so hard for us because what God gives in life is so very good. My questions still weren't answered, but, in that moment, I was graced with the gift of acceptance. I knew, without a shadow of doubt, that God gives life and that my son's life had been given back to us. I knew that God weeps with me over my father's painful dying process and is present with us always — in life, in dying, and in death. Peter spent three days in a hospital in Watertown. When he was released, the diagnosis read only, "Minor abrasions and multiple trauma." We were able to continue our vacation.

Though this happened over thirty years ago, the experience is as vivid to me now as it was on that August day in the Canadian Rockies. God touched my heart and held me, even as I held our son. My questions were subsumed in the awesome presence of God-with-me and the assurance that, finally, God's gracious presence and care is all that really matters.

God Spoke To Me

Come and see what God has done: he is awesome in his deeds among mortals. He turned the sea into dry land; they passed through the river on foot. There we rejoiced in him, who rules by his might forever, whose eyes keep watch on the nations — let the rebellious not exalt themselves. Bless our God, O peoples, let the sound of his praise be heard, who has kept us among the living and has not let our feet slip. (vv. 5-9)

Sister Alice J. Giere, S.S.N.D.

My sister, Sister Joan Frances Giere, and I were on a vacation trip with our mother. We decided to take a route through the Smokey Mountain National Park. As we entered the park, the Ranger told us that we couldn't have chosen a better day, that it was as clear as it ever gets. The beauty was breathtaking. At one of the vistas we parked and got out of the car just to drink in the beauty around us. I stood looking out over the vista, admiring the many shades of green nearby. As my eyes moved across the vista and the shades of green, with muted blues and purples far off, I noticed that even on that bright day, there was a mist over the mountaintops that hid them from view. I stood for some time in silent wonder and awe for the magnificent Creator of such beauty.

It was the following day, when I returned in my imagination to that spot in prayer, that it seemed God spoke to me. It was as though God said: "When you stood at that vista, you couldn't even appreciate the beauty right before your eyes let alone the beauty far off. That's the way it is with me. You can hardly appreciate the little you know about me now, and there is so much more I want to teach you."

I have returned to that experience often since that time and I trust that Jesus continues to teach me about his love and beauty.

Larry Gjenvick

My father, Ludvig Gjenvick, immigrated to America from Germany in the early 1900s. A few years later, when the United States entered World War I, he was drafted into the U. S. Army. After basic training, his company was ordered to France, where fierce fighting was taking place between the United States and the German armed forces.

During the long journey to France, there was ample opportunity for all of the men to think about what lay ahead. They knew that the fighting was severe and that many of them might become casualties.

My father found strength and comfort in his Bible, and one day when he picked it up, it opened randomly to Psalm 91. He said a voice led him at once to verse 7, which reads, "A thousand may fall at your side, ten thousand at your right hand, but it will not come near you." My father said that at once the weight of apprehension lifted from him and he experienced peace and calm.

Upon landing in France, my father was assigned to a supply depot well behind the front lines. He believed that, for reasons he did not fully comprehend, God had spoken directly to him through scripture to reassure him and protect him in the days ahead.

In the early 1930s, our family, which consisted of my father, mother, brother, sister, and me, lived in a home with no central heating. My father and mother slept in the one bedroom on the first floor, and we three children slept in bedrooms on the second floor. In the winter, a kerosene heater was used in the upstairs to take the chill from the rooms.

One cold winter night when we were all asleep, my father relates that he had a dream, a vision, where a figure seemed to be standing at the top of some stairs saying, "Come up." He awoke, but thinking it was just a dream, went back to sleep. Once again, he was wakened by the same kind of dream. But when it happened a third time, and the figure told him his children were in danger, he wakened and went upstairs, where he found the kerosene heater had malfunctioned and was spewing out deadly carbon monoxide fumes. He immediately extinguished the heater and opened the windows to let in fresh air.

There was no way he could have known or experienced the deadly carbon monoxide fumes on the first floor, and he was convinced that God had sent an angel to warn him and waken him so he could save his family from certain death.

At the beginning of my freshman year in college, I had an experience of my own. One evening, after studying late, I left a brightly lit building to return to my dormitory. Cutting across the very dark campus, I felt a hand on my shoulder that immediately stopped me in my tracks. I looked back and around me, but there was no one there. Gingerly, I felt in front of me with my foot, and there I found that one more step would have meant a fall over an unprotected wall to a drop of some 25 feet to a concrete slab below. I am convinced that, once again, God had intervened to save my life in a manner that could be explained in no other way. Thanks be to God!

In The Midst Of An Attack,
A Transformation

Connie Hays Coddington

Then Jesus told them a parable about their need
to pray always and not to lose heart. (v. 1)

The telephone rang in my motel room in El Salvador. When I answered it, I heard the voice of the young man who, just a couple of days before, had abducted me and attempted to rape me. He had found out the number of my room because he worked in the motel. Now he was asking me if he could take me to dinner at the restaurant in the motel.

My first response was, "You've got to be kidding!" After all, a few days earlier he had tried to attack me, and although God had saved me during that experience, I didn't want to knowingly put myself in danger again. Still, questions kept coming to my mind: Have you been healed of fear and anger toward this man or not? Did you see him as the image and likeness of God or not? Has he changed since the encounter? Is the healing complete? The answer came immediately: Yes! That is why I answered, "I will go to dinner with you."

The Psalmist assures us that God is "a very present help in trouble" (Psalm 46:1). God is always with us, and his presence is practical — the help we get from him is tangible. Thinking of the children of Israel wandering in the wilderness, the Psalmist sang, "Then they cried unto the Lord in their trouble, and he delivered them out of their distresses" (Psalm 107:6).

Both before and since those words were written down, individuals around the globe have experienced deliverance by God in one way or another. I know that he is always with us because he helped me when that young man was attacking me. I share this experience with you so that it may strengthen your trust in God.

It all began shortly after I graduated from college. A woman from my church invited me to join her on a trip to El Salvador. She was to be the guide for a tour group. I was thrilled to have such an opportunity and looked forward to an adventurous trip. When we first entered the country, I was struck by the poverty and civil unrest, and it was clear that war was brewing. I prayed to know how I might help.

One evening, after dinner with a family from Nicaragua, the young man who had driven us back to our motel asked me to stay in the car for a moment as the others were getting out. I thought he was going to park the car in the nearby lot, but he proceeded to exit the lot and drive down a quiet country road.

He did not respond to my questions about where we were going or to my request that he take me back to my motel. Fear gripped me. I reached out to God in prayer, but the fear kept me from feeling his presence. When we got to a small country motel, the man dragged me out of the car into a room.

Once inside, I was able to separate myself from him and began talking with him about my religion. I briefly explained what Christian Science was. I explained how important it was to me and how I desired to live by its standards. I spoke to him about man's spirituality and goodness and about God's love for his creation. He probably thought my comments were unusual, under the circumstances, but this was what came to my mind.

I tried to reason with him and to explain what he had in mind was wrong. After talking for about fifteen minutes, I requested once more that he take me back to my motel.

Instead, he attacked me. I turned to God with all my heart. The first thought that came to me, as I wrestled to keep the man away, was the explanation of angels from *Science and Health* by Mary Baker Eddy. Mrs. Eddy writes: "Angels. God's thoughts passing to man; spiritual intuitions, pure and perfect; the inspiration of goodness, purity and immortality, counteracting all evil, sensuality, and morality" (p. 581).

I knew God's thoughts were not only passing to me, but were also being communicated to this man in a way he could understand. This time, in the midst of fear, I felt God's presence.

As I continued to listen for spiritual insights, the idea came to pray the Lord's Prayer aloud. When I came to the line, "Forgive us our debts, as we forgive our debtors," it dawned on me that I needed to truly forgive this man and not be angry or resentful toward him.

It might seem impossible to do this under the circumstances, but this insight reminded me of man's actual spirituality and the importance of affirming this, regardless of what was happening at the moment. I realized that I needed to see this man as made in the image and likeness of God and that I needed to do this now, not some time later. In reality, he was good, pure, and innocent, the way God created him.

The next idea that came to mind was from a poem by Mrs. Eddy titled, "Mother's Evening Prayer." The line reads, "His arm encircles me, and mine, and all" (Poem, 4). God's mothering love was encircling me as well as the man. God's protecting love was present, even though I still needed to fight off the aggression.

Then there came a moment when it felt as though there was no more physical strength left in me. So I spoke to God: "Father, I can't fight anymore: You take over." I stopped resisting. You might say I yielded to God rather than to the man. At the very instant I quit wrestling, the man stopped his abuse. The attack ended. God had helped me, and the man. The man said, "You really are an angel." That's all he said, and he immediately took me back to my motel.

I didn't think I was an angel. But angels had been present. They were God's messages leading both of us to freedom.

Shortly thereafter, as I read, I came across the following from *The First Church of Christ Scientist* and *Miscellany* by Mary Baker Eddy: "Remember, thou canst be brought into no condition, be it ever so severe, where Love has not been before thee and where its tender lesson is not awaiting thee. Therefore, despair not nor murmur, for that which seeketh to save, to heal, and to deliver will guide thee, if thou seekest this guidance" (pp. 149-150).

I understood that I need not despair or murmur over the experience. Even when human encounters such as this one appear to be threatening and fear-filled, we can trust God to help us. And there does not need to be any kind of lingering after-effect. God is able to remove even the memory of such an experience. I saw so clearly that God had been present the whole time, keeping me safe.

My conviction of God's presence was what made me able to go to dinner with this young man after the attack. While we were eating, he told me of the tremendous challenges in his life and his country. He felt he would soon have to go to war. I spoke to him of a book that I was certain would help him: *Science and Health and the Key to the Scriptures* by Mary Baker Eddy. I assured him that it would give him an understanding of God, of his relationship to God, and of his safety in God's presence. I didn't have an extra book with me, but I promised to send him a copy of the Spanish translation of this book when I returned to the United States. And I did. He promised he would read it.

After dinner, he wanted me to meet his dad. I must admit that I hesitated a moment, but then I agreed to go with him. As I heard them speak to each other in Spanish, a language unknown to me, I felt the deep love between them. The dad was so sincere, kind, and humble. He had worked hard all his life for very little remuneration. But the love I felt in his presence was indescribable. I can still feel it today, many years later. This country had a richness I had been unable to see before meeting this man's father. And now I perceived how better to pray for this part of the world.

From his dad's house, the young man immediately took me back to my motel, and we parted ways with a handshake. That was twenty years ago.

This experience changed my life. It gave me a confident trust in God, because it provided rock-solid proof of his care. From the moment I discovered God's power and presence, I knew I could trust anything to him. If God was here for me when I most needed him, he would always be there for me.

God is our help always, and in times of trouble, we and our loved ones can experience that help through our prayers. No matter how far we may be from home, family, or friends, God is with us. God will help us, if we turn to him. This I know.

You Don't Depend On People

Larry Winebrenner

When deeds of iniquity overwhelm us, you forgive our transgressions. Happy are those whom you choose and bring near to live in your courts. We shall be satisfied with the goodness of your house, your holy temple. (vv. 3-4)

Names and places in the following account have been changed to protect the guilty.

Sadie was a schoolteacher in Smalltown, Wisconsin, about fifty years ago. She attended Smalltown Methodist Church. Her home sat just outside the town limits.

In the county were a dozen or so one-room schools and several more that had multiple classes meeting together. It was Sadie's dream to consolidate the schools in the county to provide better resources for the educational process. Most of her neighbors, however, loved their little local one-room schools and were not very helpful in her drive to consolidate. Sadie was indefatigable and worked with the county school board and anyone who would listen to her dream. Eventually, she was successful and a large, well-equipped consolidated school was built in Smalltown, much to the chagrin of those who opposed it.

One night Sadie's house caught fire. She tried to douse the flames, but the fire got out of control. The Smalltown Volunteer Fire Department responded to a call made by one of Sadie's neighbors. The fire truck drove right up to the Smalltown town limits and stopped some twenty feet away from the house. Instead of going to work extinguishing the fire, these good volunteer fire department church people sat on the hood of their truck and watched the house burn.

Sadie went from person to person in the crowd, pleading, "Everything I own is in that house. Please help me save it. At least, help me get some of my things out of the house." The good church people watching the fire said things like, "Why don't you ask the school board to help you?" and "Neighbors help neighbors, but you didn't think about that when you were bent and determined on consolidating our schools." They watched her house burn to the ground, then left her standing beside the smoking ruins in her nightgown as they returned to their homes.

But there's more to the story. Sadie did not move away. She was in church the following Sunday in her regular place. She continued to attend church there and taught school in Smalltown. She retired from teaching when she was seventy years old, and the school had a great celebration, honoring her as the founder of their great school. When she was 75 years old, the church gave her a testimonial as one of the church pillars. She was still active at the age of 86, when I served the church there. She told me the story (confirmed by several church members) and said, "You don't depend on people in life. You simply seek God's help, and he [sic] will provide."

Almost In Heaven

*I, Daniel, saw in my vision by night the four winds
of heaven stirring up the great sea, and four great
beasts came up out of the sea, different from one
another.* (v. 2)

John Sumwalt

In 1977, about ten years before she died, I asked my grandmother, Nellie Jane Kittle Sumwalt, then in her early eighties, if
she would allow me to tape record some of her family stories.
Grandma had plenty to tell. She told me about my great-great-grandmother, Catherine Isbell, who with her three oldest sons claimed
640 acres of Black Jack woods in the Oklahoma land rush of 1889:
160 acres each, as the Homestead Act allowed. They immediately
set about clearing some of the timber so they could plant crops,
and they began to build a house. It was a combination dugout, like
the sod houses they were accustomed to in Kansas, and logs, which
had been a rarity in the prairie country from which they had come.
In a few years there was a general store, which also served as the
post office, a church, and eventually a school. Catherine was the
moving force behind all of the building — especially the church.
She insisted that there be a place for the children to attend worship
and Sunday school.

Catherine never missed an opportunity to witness to her faith:
to tell how God had blessed her throughout her life. All of her extra
money was sent to missions. When Catherine visited her grandchildren, she always held what she called "family worship." She
would gather everyone around her and tell stories from the Bible,
and then, as Grandma tells it, "We would all join in singing the old
gospel hymns that were her favorites." Grandma said, "My folks
were not much for going to church, but when Grandma Catherine

came, she took my oldest brother Elmer and me to church every Sunday. Pa let us drive the horse and the spring wagon to church by ourselves after Grandma Catherine had gone home. One Sunday the wagon got stuck in the mud as we were crossing the creek. That was the end of going to church for a while, but Elmer and I never forgot what we had learned."

There were not many doctors in that part of the country in those days, so Catherine became the community midwife. She helped to deliver over 100 babies in her time. She always prayed during the deliveries and the Lord always answered her prayers. Catherine was very proud of the fact that she never lost a mother or a baby.

My great-great-grandmother Catherine died of pneumonia at the age of 83. The way Grandma told it, she was out making garden on a cold day when she shouldn't have been. It had rained the night before, and she crawled around on the damp ground and took sick. She was unconscious by the time her daughter Liza and grandson Elmer arrived from Texhoma. They called the doctor, and when he arrived he gave her a shot, which revived her. When she came to, she was angry. She raised her head up, looked around at everyone and said, "Ohhh, I was almost in heaven! I could see across the river; I could see over there and it was beautiful. And then the devil came along and poked his spear in my arm, and here I am back in the world!"

When Grandma finished telling this and several other stories, I knew something about myself that I hadn't known before. I knew where my faith had come from: from my great-great-grandmother, handed down through my grandmother to me.

Editor's Note: My grandmother Nellie had a similar near-death vision in the early 1980s a few years before she died. My aunt Ruth tells the following story which she heard in a telephone call from her brother, and my late uncle, Lawrence Sumwalt.

Ruth Sumwalt Cummings

My mother, Nellie Jane Kittle Sumwalt, had a fall while living in her little apartment in Richland Center. She lay on the floor a good, long while. She kept tapping on the floor with her cane, hoping to get the people in the apartment below her to hear. Evidently they were gone and couldn't hear her. She said she died while she lay there on the floor, and she saw her mother and sister, who told her to go back. I think it was her daughter-in-law's mother, Leona Long, who found her and got her help.

Dreams

Gail C. Ingle

For there is still a vision for the appointed time; it speaks of the end, and does not lie. If it seems to tarry, wait for it; it will surely come, it will not delay. (v. 3)

Several times in my life I have had precognitive dreams. It was not until a later time that I realized what the dreams foreshadowed. This past summer was one of those times.

I was having difficulty breathing due to asthma and bronchitis, but I continued to smoke two packs of cigarettes a day. I had smoked for forty years and was not about to quit. I had tried to quit once before, but was unable to stop. I loved smoking and hated it when anyone told me I "should really quit." On July 19, an "ozone action day," I was outside doing yard work: obviously something a person with asthma and bronchitis should not do. But I was stubborn and I wanted the yard to look perfect for the family party I was to host that Saturday.

When I awoke Saturday morning, I could barely breathe. I asked my neighbor to take me to the pharmacy to get a prescription for my bronchitis. When we got there, the pharmacist could tell I was having trouble breathing. He told my neighbor to take me to a doctor immediately.

I went to my regular clinic and was seen by a new physician. He gave me a nebulizing treatment that should have helped my breathing. However, it did not because I was in respiratory failure. The doctor told me I would have to go to the Intensive Care Unit at the hospital or I would die. I told him I was going home to make a phone call to cancel my party. He reiterated that I would die if I didn't go to Intensive Care. I told him I would go home because I wanted to make a call to cancel the party, when what I really wanted to do was smoke. Despite having great difficulty breathing, I smoked one cigarette on the way home, one while I made the phone call to cancel the party, and one on the way to Intensive Care.

That afternoon, while I was in my hospital bed receiving oxygen, I remembered the dream I had twenty days before. In the dream, I was looking into my bedroom and saw Death walking around my bed, but he couldn't find me. This dream was enough to cause me to know that I was being given a second chance to live, that I would never be able to smoke again.

Two Bible passages have helped sustain me in what I consider to be a miracle, being smoke-free: "Death had its hands around my throat; the terrors of the grave overtook me. I saw only trouble and sorrow. Then I called on the name of the Lord: 'Please, Lord, save me.' " (Psalm 116:3, 4) and "Anyone who calls on the name of the Lord will be saved" (Acts 2:21).

Feeling God's Peace

Penny McCanles

*On the glorious splendor of your majesty, and on
your wondrous works, I will meditate.* (v. 5)

I have a place I think of when I meditate. I'm on the pier at the
cottage where we spent many summer vacations over the course of
nearly 25 years. I am lying on my stomach on the warm wood and
the water beneath the pier is sloshing gently, the sound reverberat-
ing in the wood. If I look down between the planks, I can see a
school of minnows swim past, then reverse direction suddenly and
swim just as fast in the opposite direction. A spider is weaving its
intricate web between one of the planks and the support post. Turning my head a bit, I see the leaves on the big aspen flutter, silvery,
in the breeze. A hummingbird is poised before the feeder that hangs
in the tree. It moves forward an inch or two, sips, and darts off.
Suddenly, the quiet is broken by the chatter of a mother mallard as
she leads her brood past the pier and into the patches of purple iris
growing along the shore. I smile as I observe the downy babies
upend themselves as they dive for water bugs or perhaps young
shoots. In a few moments, the mother duck rounds them up and
leads her little parade farther down the shore. Now the sun is high.
The birds are still. Nature is silent, waiting. I wait, too, feeling
God's peace.

A Narrow Escape

Jo Perry-Sumwalt

Surely God is my salvation; I will trust, and will
not be afraid, for the Lord God is my strength and
my might; he has become my salvation. (v. 2)

I was savoring one of those rare winter weekends when I am able to get away, on my own, to our little farm in southwest Wisconsin. I had spent three relaxing days working on odd jobs, shopping for supplies and furnishings, and watching movies with only our dog Eli for company. Weekends like these are special to me, not only for the freedom and solitude, but also for how happy I am to be back together with the rest of the family when they are over. Absence does, indeed, make the heart grow fonder.

The final part of my weekend was to be a forty-mile trip to visit my parents and go to worship services with my mom on Sunday morning. It was beginning to snow when I woke up and got ready to go, but I called ahead and told Mom I would pick her up in time for church.

Our farm is located in the valley, surrounded by hills. The shortest route to my parents' was over the hills to the highway, so I started out in plenty of time to travel slowly and safely. The car climbed the first ridge, past sandstone bluffs on the right and a forty-foot, unguarded drop-off on the left. I always drive that stretch of road carefully, but even with the front-wheel drive on our new car, it was obvious that I couldn't make the trip, over any more of the several ridges and valleys, safely in that snow. I thought of the dog, alone at the farm with no one to take care of him if I should make it to my parents' and be unable to get back, and I turned the car around in the driveway of the farm at the top of the hill and started back down.

The first thing I remember is being aware that the road was much more slippery going down than coming up. The second is that I was acutely aware that there was no guardrail along the side of the road with the forty-foot drop into a ravine. The snow was several inches deep by that time, and no snowplows had been through on an early Sunday morning. I instinctively began to pump my brakes to slow my speed on that steep, unguarded part of the hill. But the more I pumped, the more the car slid to the right, closer and closer to the embankment, until the front end was pointing directly toward the edge, and I knew that if I didn't stop, I would sail right over the edge and dive, nose first, into the ravine.

I had been talking to God since I started out, as I often do when I'm alone, relaying my plans to take it slow and easy, worrying about the conditions, deciding to turn around, and praying to make it safely down the hill. As my car slid nose first toward that embankment, and no adjustment in the steering made any difference, and I felt the right front tire go off the pavement onto the gravel shoulder, my plea was, "Oh, God! No! No!" and as I said it, my right foot did what I knew not to do: pressed hard on the brake, and my left foot joined it, and the steering wheel responded under my hands, and I was able to steer the car away from the edge, back onto the road.

I stopped there, in the middle of the road, with my heart pounding and my ears ringing, for at least a minute before I was able to stop shaking enough to go on. In my *mind*, I realized that I had finally done what was necessary. Our new car had antilock brakes, which are not intended to be pumped, but stepped on firmly. Never having used them before, I had forgotten that detail. But my *heart* knew that, when I was in danger, I had called out to God, and God answered my prayer. It wasn't *my* mind that made me step on the brakes with both feet, when I had been taught never to do that. I thanked God all the way back to the farm, and for hours afterward as I sat in the living room, snuggled in blankets, cuddling with the dog, safe!

Have No Anxiety

*Have no anxiety about anything, but in everything
by prayer and supplication with thanksgiving let
your requests be made known to God. And the
peace of God, which passes all understanding,
will keep your hearts and minds in Christ Jesus.*
(vv. 6-7)

Marjorie K. Evans

Many years ago, when my little son, David, was 28 months old
and my baby, Charles, was three months old, my husband deserted
us for another woman. I was shocked to my very being and utterly
devastated. I felt as if the earth had dropped from beneath my feet.

My parents invited us to live with them, so we moved to their
small town. Although they helped me with the babies, nothing
seemed to help my broken heart. As I sat in Mom's rocker and
nursed baby Charles, I read my Bible through the tears that seemed
as if they would never stop flowing. Indeed, the pain was further
compounded by little David's anguished pleas of "Buy me a daddy.
I want a daddy."

My only hope was in Jesus, so I appropriated many of the Bible
verses for myself. Some that were especially meaningful were:
"Cast all your anxieties on him, for he cares for you" (1 Peter 5:7),
"... I will never fail you nor forsake you" (Hebrews 13:5), "Fear
not, for I am with you, be not dismayed, for I am your God; I will
strengthen you, I will help you, I will uphold you with my victori-
ous right hand" (Isaiah 41:10).

Even though I appropriated those promises and many others, I
kept wondering what would happen to my babies and me. So I
worried and was distraught and blue.

Then one cold winder night I was awakened by someone calling, "Marjorie!" I thought it was my mother, for she sometimes checked to see if the babies and I were covered up.

"Mom?" I questioned, but she was not in the room, for there was no answer.

Drowsy, I turned over and was almost asleep when I again heard, "Marjorie!" This time I became wide awake.

The Lord spoke to my heart and said, "Marjorie, you are worried about many things, but you are not to be anxious for anything. Don't you remember I died on the cross for you? I suffered untold agony for you. I understand your heartache, for everything that concerns you concerns me. I want you to give me all of your cares, for I love you with an everlasting love. And I will never leave you nor forsake you. You, David, and baby Charles are all in the hollow of my hand. All you have to do is love me and trust me."

I lay awake for a long time, in complete awe, pondering all the things the Lord had told me.

After that precious experience with Jesus, the feeling of gloom and despair lifted, even though my circumstances hadn't changed. And as I continued to read my Bible and pray day after day, and week after week, my love, faith, and trust in the Lord kept increasing.

We couldn't continue to live with my parents, as Mother and Dad were not very well. Also, there were no jobs available in their small town. One day, my sister Mary called and said, "Marjorie, Ben and I have been praying about your situation. We'd like to have you move to California so I can baby sit the kiddies, and you'll be able to find a job."

After much prayer, we moved to Mary and Ben's city. We found a duplex two houses down from them, and I obtained a secretarial job and was able to ride to work with Ben.

The seven years I was alone and the sole support of my two little boys were not easy ones. I didn't make much money, there were illnesses, and sometimes I didn't know where our next meal would come from. But the Lord always provided — sometimes through friends at church, people at work, neighbors, and my sister Mary and her husband Ben.

After a couple of years, I began to date Edgar, a fine man who also attended the Single's Group at church. He liked my two young sons and always took them with us when we had afternoon dates.

One afternoon, Ed took us miniature golfing. After he left, David asked, "Mommy, why don't you ask Ed to marry you?"

"Oh, honey," I explained, "women don't ask men to marry them."

He persisted, "But, Mommy, why not? I like Ed and want him to be my daddy."

After a year and a half of dating, Ed asked me to marry him. He adopted the boys as his own. David and Charles were delighted as they finally had a daddy. Ed was a wonderful and loving husband, father, and eventually, grandfather.

On August 4, 2002, we celebrated our 42nd wedding anniversary in the intensive care unit of the acute care hospital where Ed had been confined for several months. Ed, David, and I visited, listened to gospel songs, read the Bible, and prayed. In spite of his being bedfast and having to use a voice box in his tracheotomy, Ed smiled and commented, "This has been a good anniversary."

Then a month and a half later, on September 18, Ed died. He's now in heaven with our precious Lord, whom he dearly loved and faithfully served. The days and nights are extremely lonely and sad without him. But, I know I'll see him in heaven someday, and we'll spend eternity worshiping and praising our dear Savior and Lord.

So, through the years — dire, difficult, happy, and sad — I've been in the hollow of God's hand and can truly say, "Thou dost keep him in perfect peace, whose mind is stayed on thee, because he trusts on thee" (Isaiah 26:3).

Robert Gossett

My wife Jeri and I had been planning a motor coach tour of Washington, D.C., for several months. We had been there in 1966 and were looking forward to seeing the new memorials as well as the many other sights in the area. Our anticipation and excitement were growing as the time drew nearer ... until a sniper began shooting people in the area where we would be traveling and staying. We prayed that the sniper would be caught, but that didn't happen, and Jeri's anxiety grew. She was concerned, not just that one of us could be shot, but that we couldn't really have a good time with a sniper in the area. Eight people had been killed and two wounded at the time. We had travel insurance and would receive a full refund if we cancelled for any reason. We struggled with what to do as we prayed for guidance.

I asked the men at the men's breakfast group I attended, on the Saturday before the Monday on which the trip was to begin, what they would do. They all said they would go. One of the men, Tim, suggested that I share Philippians 4:6-7 with Jeri. I was familiar with it, but I checked it later:

> *Do not worry about anything, but in everything by prayer and supplication with thanksgiving let your requests be made known to God. And the peace of God, which surpasses all understanding, will guard your hearts and your minds in Christ Jesus.*

I planned to share this with Jeri when I had time.

I had some yard work to finish in the morning and a wedding to officiate in the afternoon, so Jeri remained concerned about the trip. While the wedding party was taking pictures, I called Jeri to say everything was running late and I wouldn't be home until about 6:00 p.m. She replied, "We're going on the trip. I'll tell you about it when you get home." I could hardly wait to find out what had brought about such a dramatic change.

Jeri told me later that she had talked to her brother, who told her about two gang-related shootings in their area. "There are problems everywhere and you can't get away from them. I would go," he said. But that wasn't all.

Jeri decided to seek guidance from the Bible. She was leafing through the pages when she came upon Philippians 4:6-7. The words gave her the confidence that we can live with trust in God and not in fear of a sniper or other concern. We are not necessarily protected from every problem, of course, but we have assurance of God's presence no matter what. I didn't have to point out Tim's suggested scripture to Jeri. God did that directly, and gave us a wonderful trip.

Visions Of Christ

*He is the image of the invisible God, the firstborn
of all creation; for in him all things in heaven and
on earth were created, things visible and invisible,
whether thrones or dominions or rulers or powers
— all things have been created through him and
for him. He himself is before all things, and in him
all things hold together.* (vv. 15-17)

Linda Nafziger-Meiser

In 1982-86, my husband and I lived in the Shenandoah Valley
near Harrisonburg, Virginia. One fall day, I spontaneously decided
to use my time off from work to make applesauce, so I headed out
of town to the apple orchards in the countryside, driving our little
VW camper van. I was headed west in the left lane of a one-way
street, coming up on an out-of-state vehicle in the right lane. When
my front wheels were about even with their rear wheels, they started
to turn right across my lane into a business on the left side of the
street — right in my path. There was no time to hit the brakes; they
were right there, which in a camper van is "very" close. I screamed,
and as I braced for the crash, I clearly saw Jesus in the passenger
seat flinging out his arms to shield me from the impact. Irratio-
nally, I thought, "Of course! He's going to die instead of me, once
again." But there was no crash.

Somehow, unbelievably, their car had crossed in front of my
VW without any contact. The other driver started yelling, furious
at me for nearly causing an accident. I wordlessly pointed at the
one-way street sign and he and his passenger promptly turned even
whiter. We stared at one another, shaking our heads in disbelief
that we hadn't crashed, utterly shaken. When my legs quit shaking,
I got back into my van and drove off — and Jesus was still sitting

211

in the passenger seat. I could turn my head and look right at him and then he seemed fainter, like looking at a dim star right on. But when I looked straight ahead and saw him with my peripheral vision, he was quite clear. When I spoke to him, he did not respond verbally or audibly, but his body language was clear, giving me a profound sense of peace and compassionate love.

He didn't leave for several weeks, although the impressions grew fainter. During that time, I could always sense or see precisely where he was, never invasive but always nearby with that gentle, powerful grace and love and peace flowing from him directly into the desolate, shame-filled places within me.

At that time, I was a young wife struggling with the poisonous after-effects of childhood sexual abuse. While I had already experienced much healing, there was still much more to go, and would continue to be for many more years. But so much of my steady transformation into health since then has built on that experience — the tangible sense of Jesus' vital connection and care and concern for me. The suicidal depressions that had shaped so much of my adolescent and young adult life ended at that point.

Now, as a pastor, I take special joy in doing spiritual direction with women who have experienced sexual abuse or other childhood trauma. I tell them, when we begin meeting, that one of my primary aims in working with them in this way is to help make God's overwhelming love and care for them real and tangible. And this is as transforming for them as it has been for me.

Cynthia Kristopeit

In 1992 my life changed forever because of a divorce, and I went through some very dark and stressful years. I was beside myself with grief, fear, and anger, and since much of my life had centered upon my husband and his attaining his goals, I had forgotten who I was. I now believe that my self-worth was quite low. Being an extension of his goals and dreams did a number on reclaiming who I really was.

I prayed that God would guide me through the pain, but there were days when I didn't ever think that life would be normal again. I wondered how I could survive. My supervising elder at that time suggested the name of a Christian therapist. During one counseling session, I remember really struggling with my self-worth. The counselor asked me to close my eyes. He suggested I go in my mind to a place that I loved.

I had no difficulty with that, since there is one place in the world where I have experienced God's love again and again — Gate's Pass outside of Tucson, Arizona, in Saguaro National Monument West. My mind's eye immediately climbed up to the stone picnic pavilion that overlooks the pass down into the majesty of the Sonaran Desert valley. One sees literally thousands upon thousands of stately saguaro's for miles. I had nicknamed those saguaros "God's sentinels." I felt safe there.

After several minutes, the therapist asked me to picture someone coming to me. Instantly, I saw Jesus. He came over the rocks towards me as I looked out over the valley and we sat down on a rock together gazing at the beauty. We just sat there a long time ... Jesus and me. I felt warm and safe. After some time, Jesus looked into my eyes and he said, "You really love this spot, don't you?"

"Yes," I said.

He smiled and said, "I'm so glad, because I made it just for you."

I was stunned. As I told the therapist about my experience, I cried. Jesus didn't think I was worthless. The struggle to love ourselves, as we are loved, is an unending human struggle. But whenever I get those feelings, I relive that incredible moment ... that gift of seeing God's creation as a gift to me.

Vera Kin

Have you ever felt that the Lord was holding your hand and saying encouraging words to you? Well, I did.

"The results of the biopsy show that you have cancer."

The doctor's words hit like a bombshell. How could it be? I just sat there and did not say a word. Finally, the doctor said to me, "Are you okay?"

And I replied, "No, I am not okay. I am a basket case." I had gone to the doctor's office alone when they called for me to hear the results of a biopsy on a lump I had discovered.

He said, "I want you to know that, no matter how hard it is for you to hear this, it is also very hard for me to have to tell you." Some of my friends can hardly believe that that man, noted for being very, very hard-nosed, would even be able to say that. But he did. He offered surgery and an irreversible colostomy. Oh my!

My social worker friend, Millie, said later that she wished she had gone with me, and wondered why I hadn't asked her to go along. It was such devastating news, I didn't even want to talk about it. I couldn't tell my four sons, but my friend kept after me. Finally, one Sunday afternoon I called each one and asked if they could come to see me "right now."

It was only a short time until they all arrived, with some adult grandchildren along. It struck me how easy it was to get all of us together, when so many times we had tried to plan an anniversary dinner and it seemed impossible to find a time suitable to all.

One son said, "Maybe they can just cut out that part and patch you up." My engineer grandson told me, "You know they are all electricians and that is how they fix things." All the sons and wives and families were very, very supportive. One daughter-in-law told me, "Now you just fight this!"

My surgeon, Dr. Fox, said he was reading up about my case and it was unusual. They only see a couple like it each year. But he offered a possible cure with radiation and chemotherapy, with a 50-50 chance of cure, and if it did work, they would not have to do a colostomy. Well, with those odds, I jumped at the chance, of course. And if it didn't work, they could still do the colostomy.

I was not told that the radiation would permanently damage all of the skin in the area, nor that the chemo itself would almost kill me. Later, in the ensuing weeks of fogged consciousness, I do remember hearing the chemo doctor yelling out to someone, "I can't give her any more chemotherapy."

For the radiation therapy, I was measured and received some tattoos where the radiation was to be aimed. After the specialist pushed and pulled and nudged my body into the exact position it needed to be, I was cautioned to be very still and not move. During the times I received radiation (I cannot remember how many), now hear this, my Lord, in a white robe, stood right beside me and all the time held my hand to help me be still. And he told me I was going to get well. It was all so calm and comforting to me, and I never doubted for a minute. As sick as I was during several months of recovery, I remembered that he said I would get well. And I did.

All I can think, even today, is, "Thank you, God, for being with me, and thank you for the people you gave me to help me. And thank you for this beautiful day in your beautiful world."

I have told you this time and again. If a person were in a rapture as great at Saint Paul once experienced and learned that her neighbor were in need of a cup of soup, it would be best to withdraw from the rapture and give the person the soup she needs.

Meister Eckhart

This is the second in a series of three books of *Vision Stories*. If you have a story to share, please send it to John Sumwalt at 2044 Forest Street, Wauwatosa, Wisconsin 53213, or fax to 414-453-0702, or e-mail to jsumwalt@naspa.net. Phone 414-257-1228.

Matthew Fox, *Meditations with Meister Eckhardt* (Santa Fe: Bear and Company, 1982), p. 71.

U.S. / Canadian Lectionary Comparison

The following index shows the correlation between the Sundays and special days of the church year as they are titled or labeled in the Revised Common Lectionary published by the Consultation On Common Texts and used in the United States (the reference used for this book) and the Sundays and special days of the church year as they are titled or labeled in the Revised Common Lectionary used in Canada.

Revised Common Lectionary	Canadian Revised Common Lectionary
Advent 1	Advent 1
Advent 2	Advent 2
Advent 3	Advent 3
Advent 4	Advent 4
Christmas Eve	Christmas Eve
Nativity Of The Lord / Christmas Day	The Nativity Of Our Lord
Christmas 1	Christmas 1
January 1 / Holy Name of Jesus	January 1 / The Name Of Jesus
Christmas 2	Christmas 2
Epiphany Of The Lord	The Epiphany Of Our Lord
Baptism Of The Lord / Epiphany 1	The Baptism Of Our Lord / Proper 1
Epiphany 2 / Ordinary Time 2	Epiphany 2 / Proper 2
Epiphany 3 / Ordinary Time 3	Epiphany 3 / Proper 3
Epiphany 4 / Ordinary Time 4	Epiphany 4 / Proper 4
Epiphany 5 / Ordinary Time 5	Epiphany 5 / Proper 5
Epiphany 6 / Ordinary Time 6	Epiphany 6 / Proper 6
Epiphany 7 / Ordinary Time 7	Epiphany 7 / Proper 7
Epiphany 8 / Ordinary Time 8	Epiphany 8 / Proper 8
Transfiguration Of The Lord / Last Sunday After Epiphany	The Transfiguration Of Our Lord / Last Sunday After Epiphany
Ash Wednesday	Ash Wednesday
Lent 1	Lent 1
Lent 2	Lent 2
Lent 3	Lent 3
Lent 4	Lent 4
Lent 5	Lent 5
Passion / Palm Sunday (Lent 6)	Passion / Palm Sunday
Holy / Maundy Thursday	Holy / Maundy Thursday
Good Friday	Good Friday
Resurrection Of The Lord / Easter	The Resurrection Of Our Lord

Easter 2	Easter 2
Easter 3	Easter 3
Easter 4	Easter 4
Easter 5	Easter 5
Easter 6	Easter 6
Ascension Of The Lord	The Ascension Of Our Lord
Easter 7	Easter 7
Day Of Pentecost	The Day Of Pentecost
Trinity Sunday	The Holy Trinity
Proper 4 / Pentecost 2 / O T 9*	Proper 9
Proper 5 / Pent 3 / O T 10	Proper 10
Proper 6 / Pent 4 / O T 11	Proper 11
Proper 7 / Pent 5 / O T 12	Proper 12
Proper 8 / Pent 6 / O T 13	Proper 13
Proper 9 / Pent 7 / O T 14	Proper 14
Proper 10 / Pent 8 / O T 15	Proper 15
Proper 11 / Pent 9 / O T 16	Proper 16
Proper 12 / Pent 10 / O T 17	Proper 17
Proper 13 / Pent 11 / O T 18	Proper 18
Proper 14 / Pent 12 / O T 19	Proper 19
Proper 15 / Pent 13 / O T 20	Proper 20
Proper 16 / Pent 14 / O T 21	Proper 21
Proper 17 / Pent 15 / O T 22	Proper 22
Proper 18 / Pent 16 / O T 23	Proper 23
Proper 19 / Pent 17 / O T 24	Proper 24
Proper 20 / Pent 18 / O T 25	Proper 25
Proper 21 / Pent 19 / O T 26	Proper 26
Proper 22 / Pent 20 / O T 27	Proper 27
Proper 23 / Pent 21 / O T 28	Proper 28
Proper 24 / Pent 22 / O T 29	Proper 29
Proper 25 / Pent 23 / O T 30	Proper 30
Proper 26 / Pent 24 / O T 31	Proper 31
Proper 27 / Pent 25 / O T 32	Proper 32
Proper 28 / Pent 26 / O T 33	Proper 33
Christ The King (Proper 29 / O T 34)	Proper 34 / Christ The King / Reign Of Christ
Reformation Day (October 31)	Reformation Day (October 31)
All Saints' Day (November 1 or 1st Sunday in November)	All Saints' Day (November 1)
Thanksgiving Day (4th Thursday of November)	Thanksgiving Day (2nd Monday of October)

*O T = Ordinary Time

Contributors

Lucinda Alwa, an ordained deacon in the Wisconsin Conference United Methodist Church, served as pastor of Little Prairie UMC from 1995-2002. She is currently on leave of absence and is teaching Classical Mythology at Northern Illinois University. She and her husband, Rajesh, have a daughter, Bethany. They share their home in Lake Geneva, Wisconsin, with five cats and a Dalmatian.

Theonia Amenda is a retired Diaconal Minister in The United Methodist Church. She continues in ministry in the area of Spiritual Formation as the leader of a Three Year Covenant Community and retreats, a speaker, and a spiritual director. Write to her at: 3612 Birnamwood Drive, Slinger, Wisconsin 53086. Phone: 262-644-8385.

Janet Beltman is a retiree of the YMCA of Metropolitan Milwaukee and a lifelong member of Perseverance Presbyterian Church in Milwaukee, Wisconsin, where she was ordained an Elder in 1977 and Deacon in 1994. Since 1990 she has been responsible for preparing the meal her church serves at the Agape Community Center in Milwaukee. Since her retirement in 1984, she has served as an officer of the YMCA Retirees' Wisconsin Chapter, along with various other volunteer commitments.

Christal Bindrich is pastor of the Mayville United Methodist Church in Mayville, Wisconsin. She welcomes opportunities to talk about mystical experiences. She can be reached at 307 N. Main Street, Mayville, Wisconsin 53050. Phone: 920-387-4711.
E-mail: bindrich@internetwis.com.

Lois Rae Carlson is a lifelong Christian Scientist, a member of Second Church of Christ, Scientist in Evanston, Illinois. As a Christian Science practitioner, she has been in the full-time healing ministries since 1976. She teaches an annual class in healing. A well-known writer, her articles can be found in the *Christian Science*

Journal, Sentinel and *Monitor*, as well as on the website: www.spirituality.com.

Rebecca Coan-Henderleiter is a Native American Catholic and attends the Congregation of the Great Spirit in Milwaukee, Wisconsin. She is a recovering addict, clean since 1989. Her life is devoted to her sons, Tony and Matthew, and to working with addicts and mentally ill persons seeking recovery.
E-mail: henderleiter@cs.com.

David E. Cobb is Senior Minister at Community Christian Church (Disciples of Christ) in Richardson, Texas. He has published articles in *Habitat World* and *Biblical Preaching Journal,* and has authored *Let Every Tongue Confess*, a study curriculum for the Apostolic Faith Study for the World Council of Churches and Order Commission. He currently serves as Vice President for Christian Unity and Interfaith Relations of the Greater Dallas Community of Churches and as an instructor of Disciples History and Polity for the North Texas and Trinity Brazos Areas of the Christian Church (Disciples of Christ).

Connie Hays Coddington has been serving the healing ministry as a Christian Science practitioner for the past twenty years. She is a member of First Church of Christ, Scientist, Brookfield, Wisconsin, and also a member of The Mother Church, The First Church of Christ, Scientist in Boston, Massachusetts. Connie is on the Christian Science Committee on Publication for Wisconsin. In this capacity she writes regularly for the media and works with the state legislature to preserve and advance religious freedoms. She has written for *The Christian Science Sentinel, El Heraldo de la Christian Science, The Milwaukee Journal Sentinel, The Waukesha Freeman, CNI Newspapers,* and *The La Crosse Tribune.* You may reach Connie at 13500 Watertown Plank Road, Suite 101, Elm Grove, Wisconsin 53122-2200. Phone: 262-796-1961. Fax: 262-796-1971. E-mail: ccoddington@aol.com.

Ruth Sumwalt Cummings is a former teacher, mother of three, and grandmother of two, who resides in Raleigh, North Carolina, with her husband, George. She is a member of Highland United Methodist Church, and is known for her singing.

Mary DeMuth grew up in the Pacific Northwest and now lives in Texas with her husband and three young children. She has designed and produced four non-profit newsletters and has been published in the *Marriage Partnership and Discipleship Journal*. She writes a weekly column for her local suburban newspaper and is working on her first novel. Her husband, Patrick, is attending Dallas Theological Seminary. E-mail: demuthtx@att.net.

Lee Domann is a United Methodist minister appointed by the Kansas East Conference to music ministry. He is a singer/songwriter/storyteller and plays in churches throughout the United States and Canada. One pastor calls him "Garrison Keillor with a Guitar." His website is www.LeeDomann.com.

Mary Downing is published daily in the homes of friends and family members living throughout the United States. A prolific letter writer, Mary still views the mailbox as a wonderful way to convey thoughts and dreams and updates on life in Port Washington, Wisconsin, the place she has called home for the past thirty years. You may write to her at 204 W. Jackson Street, Port Washington, Wisconsin 53074. E-mail: lucdowning@att.net.

Kris Drollinger is a medical transcriber who lives quietly in suburban Milwaukee with her husband, daughter, and two cats. They are members of Trinity Pilgrim United Methodist Church.

David Eaton is pastor of Zion Covenant Church in Ellsworth, Wisconsin. His father, Kenneth Eaton, at the age of 78, is still farming the land mentioned in his story. David and his wife, Shawnee, have three sons, Tim, Kyle, and Scott. They have served four congregations in the Evangelical Covenant Church over the past 22 years.

Vickie Eckoldt is a member of Wauwatosa Avenue United Methodist Church in Wauwatosa, Wisconsin. She and her husband, Al, have been married for 35 years and have one grown daughter, Pam, and a grandson, Travis. One of Vickie's visions, titled "A Life Redeemed," was published in *Vision Stories: True Accounts of Visions, Angels, and Healing Miracles.*

Marjorie K. Evans, a former elementary school teacher, is now a freelance writer with many published articles in Christian magazines, teacher's publications, and Sunday school papers. Her devotional articles have been included in sixteen devotional books. She attends Calvary Chapel of Lake Forest, California. Marjorie enjoys her two fine sons, a lovely daughter-in-law, and four neat grandchildren. She also enjoys reading and raising orchids. She resides at 4162 Fireside Circle, Irvine, California 92604.

Judith M. Evenden is a graduate of Queen's University (BA in Music and Education) and Queen's Theological College (Master of Divinity) in Kingston, Ontario, and a member of the Order of Ministry in the United Church of Canada. Judith currently serves the congregation of Fairbank United in Toronto. While this is her first story to be published, in 1990 she released a recording of all original music titled *Rainbow Tales.*

Barbara Frank lives in Port Washington, Wisconsin, and attends Grand Avenue United Methodist Church. A widow, Barbara is the mother of three sons and grandmother of two. She works for a sales promotion agency.

Wayne Frank is a Milwaukee native who served as an alderman on the city's south side for 27 years, between 1973 and 2000. Currently, he is a professional playwright with four plays that have been produced in Milwaukee. His most recent work is on the story of Joan of Arc.

Sara Jan Garza is a lifelong member of First United Methodist Church in Fort Madison, Iowa. She graduated in 1999 from the

School of Lay Ministry and has been engaged in pulpit supply since 1995, preaching in churches of various denominations. Jan teaches an adult Sunday school class and represents her church in Parish Partners, a group of five churches of different denominations. Her full-time job is as an accountant for Lee County. She and her husband, Vincent, are the parents of three children: Robin, who died in 1978, Sierra, 21, and Christopher, 15. E-mail: sara_jang@yahoo.com.

Aba Gayle attended Oconomowoc and Shorewood High Schools and the University of Wisconsin, and currently resides in Silverton, Oregon, although she considers Northern California to be home. Her two children are physicians, and she has four grandchildren. After careers as a homemaker and in health insurance, Aba Gayle now devotes her time to the Catherine Blount Foundation, which she founded to spread the healing lessons of forgiveness. She has been featured in numerous magazines and newspapers around the world. She presents workshops titled "The Healing Power of Forgiveness" and speaks in schools and churches. She currently attends church at the Living Enrichment Center in Wilsonville, Oregon, where she is active in their prison ministry. The Catherine Blount Foundation's website is www.catherineblountfdn.org.

Alice J. Giere, S.S.N.D., felt her calling to become a teaching Sister at a college junior. She worked one year after graduation, then entered religious life to become a School Sister of Notre Dame. After teaching junior high students and serving as a school administrator for forty years, Alice worked as a secretary to the dean in a local Catholic university for nearly ten years before becoming semi-retired. She now does volunteer teaching and massage therapy.

Phil Gilman, a retired professional land surveyor, has been a member of the Presbyterian Church (USA) since 1967. He has been ordained as both an elder and a deacon, and has served on various committees of the church and of Monmouth Presbytery for many years. Since his retirement, God has led him into ministry to the church through writing "Phil's Musings" on the weekly Rev.Comm.Lectionary readings which are posted on several pastors' e-lists.

Larry Gjenvick was born in Minneapolis, Minnesota. He now lives in Pewaukee, Wisconsin, and attends St. Matthew's Lutheran Church in Wauwatosa, Wisconsin. A graduate of St. Olaf College in Minnesota, Larry served in the Navy during WWII. Now retired, he is active in his church and numerous hobbies.

Robert Gossett is pastor of Grand Avenue United Methodist Church in Port Washington, Wisconsin, where he lives with his wife, Jeri. They have two grown children, Tim and Christina. Bob has had several articles published in *Marriage* magazine. His personal "Encounter With God" was published in *Vision Stories: True Accounts of Visions, Angels, and Healing Miracles.* Bob plans to retire in July 2003 to pursue part-time visitation ministry and other interests in the Milwaukee area. Fax: 262-284-9478. E-mail: gaumc@milwpc.com.

Elaine Klemm Grau is a retired psychotherapist, MSSW, UWM, spiritual director, MA, Sacred Heart School of Theology, Hales Corners, Wisconsin, Sacred Heart Congregation, Racine, Wisconsin, Eucharistic Minister, catechist, lector, communion presider, and President of Hickory Hollow Development. Contact her at: 4835 Richmond Drive, Racine, Wisconsin 53406. Phone: 262-637-2277. E-mail: egrau@execpc.com.

Bonnie Compton Hanson is the author of the *Ponytail Girls* books for girls, plus other books, poems, stories, and articles, including stories in three *Chicken Soup for the Soul* books. Write to her at 3330 S. Lowell Street, Santa Ana, California 92707. Phone: 714-751-7824: E-mail: bonnieh1@worldnet.att.net.

Britney-Lee Joy Hessel is a freshman at Hamilton High School in Milwaukee and a member of Christ United Methodist Church in Greenfield, where she sings in the choir and serves as a youth representative on the Church Council. Britney-Lee plays trumpet and is the author of a children's play, which was performed in her church's Christmas program.

Lori Hetzel attends Christ United Methodist Church in Greenfield, Wisconsin. She has been married to her very best friend, Karl, for 14 years, and is currently a stay-at-home mom, raising their newly adopted daughter, Delany, 2 1/2, and their two sons, Logan and Connor. Lori's story "Consolation" appeared in *Vision Stories: True Accounts of Visions, Angels, and Healing Miracles.*
E-mail: lhetzel@wi.rr.com.

Laura Hoff works as Coordinator of Shared Ministries and Christian Nurture at First United Methodist Church in Baraboo, Wisconsin. She is active in the Wisconsin Chapter of the Christian Educators Fellowship. Laura, her husband, and their three children live in Stoughton, Wisconsin. E-mail: lhoff@wisconsinumc.org.

Bill Hoglund pastors the First Congregational United Church of Christ in Downers Grove, Illinois, with his clergy spouse, Laura. He has a Certificate of Gerontology and served as a chaplain and health care administrator. He is engaged in Improv and Sketch Comedy in Chicago, and likes to pretend he's a golfer, too.
E-mail: revbill@mindspring.com.

Claire Hunston lives with her husband on the sheltered side of Vancouver Island, off the west coast of British Columbia. She had a sobering brush with death in an automobile accident in 1968. That and her husband's illness have resulted in frequent conversations about the process of dying. She now participates in an e-mail study of Julian of Norwich. A retired teacher, who worked mostly as an ESL teacher to children and adults from many countries, Claire still enjoys tutoring. She is on the pastoral care team of the United Church of Canada congregation where she attends and sings in the choir, helps with the Interfaith Soup Kitchen, facilitates a Parkinson's Support Group, and writes letters for Amnesty International.

Gail C. Ingle has her Master's Degree in education and teaches special education in the Waukesha, Wisconsin, school system, where she has taught for the past twenty years. She enjoys writing, and some of her poetry has been published. Gail is a member of the Genesee United Congregational Church.

Vanessa Bruce Ingold says people often tell her, "You're a walking miracle!" She and her husband, Greg, live in Fullerton, California, and attend Capo Beach Calvary Chapel. You may reach her at: JCnessa@aol.com.

Susan D. Jamison is an ordained elder in the Central Pennsylvania Conference of The United Methodist Church. In addition to serving in parish ministry, she has worked as a counselor with survivors of sexual abuse and domestic violence, and as a parent educator. E-mail: sjamison@evenlink.com.

Jeanne Jones is pastor of Ash Creek and Willow Valley United Methodist Churches near Richland Center, Wisconsin. One of her stories appeared in *Vision Stories: True Accounts of Visions, Angels, and Healing Miracles*. Write to her at: P.O. Box 153, Sextonville, Wisconsin 53584. E-mail: paradigm@mwt.net.

Patricia C. Joyce is retired from hotel/restaurant/convention business in Virginia Beach, Virginia, and enjoys the stimulus and contacts she makes as a local licensed tour guide. When she is not attending her mother in the nursing home, Pat worships at neighboring churches. Write to her at: 1066 Charity Drive, Virginia Beach, Virginia 23455. Fax: 757-464-2893.

Joy L. Kilby grew up on a farm in Vinton, Iowa. She has three sons. Joy married Downer Kilby in 1996. She presently works with disabled adults. Her passion is Bible mystery and the supernatural. Her personal testimony is Job 33, dreams, and visions.

Vera Kin retired two years ago, at the age of 83, after 27 years of clerical work for Waukesha County Health and Human Services.

She is a member of First United Methodist Church of Waukesha, Wisconsin, chairperson for adult fellowship, leader of a United Methodist Women's Circle, and active in three other circles. She feels blessed to be frequently asked to be a spiritual guide to confirmation students. Vera and her late husband had seven children, fifteen grandchildren, and fifteen great-grandchildren. She authored the book, *Times of My Life*, about her experiences, including making it through the Great Depression.

Cheryl Kirking has led her "Musical Celebrations of Worship" family concerts and women's conferences at hundreds of churches across the country. Drawing upon her professional background in lay and children's ministry, education, and performance, she weaves original songs, humor, and storytelling while maintaining a deep integrity with scripture. She has recorded six CDs on the Mill Pond Music label and is the author of the books *Ripples of Joy* (Shaw Publishers), *All Is Calm, All Is Bright: True Stories of Christmas* (Baker Books), and *Teacher, You're An A+* (Harvest House), available at bookstores nationwide or on her website. For information about bringing Cheryl to your church, contact Ripples of Encouragement™, P.O. Box 525, Lake Mills, Wisconsin 53551. Phone: 920-648-8959. Website: www.cherylkirking.com.

Cynthia Kristopeit, a graduate of Garrett-Evangelical Theological Seminary, is a member of the Wisconsin Conference of The United Methodist Church and currently serves the Delevan United Methodist Church. She has contributed to *Word and Witness*, a homiletic resource tool, and has authored several issues. She has also had one of her sermons published in *Seasons of Preaching*, Liturgical Publications, New Berlin, Wisconsin. Her other published works include poems and an essay titled "Women and Their Call to the Priesthood." She is the mother of two children: Jennifer Bruno and Christian Ruud.

Lisa Lancaster was ordained as a pastor in the Presbyterian Church (USA) in 1987. After pastoring a church for four years, she answered a call to specialized ministry as a chaplain, becoming Board

Certified in the Association of Professional Chaplains in 1994. For the past ten years, she has served as Chaplain/Director of Pastoral Care at CentraState Health Care System. She has taught on the topic "High Death Awareness" at a national conference. Lisa and her husband, Richard, a research meteorologist, live in Millstone Township, New Jersey, with their "four-legged children" (one cat, one dog), and enjoy traveling.

Debi Lyerly Lawson is the wife of Tom and mother of Bill, 18 and B. J., 17. She works as a customer service associate for BellSouth Telecommunications, and has had some of her poetry published. Debi and her family live in Alabama with their two dogs, Rusty and Harley, and "a bunch of cats."
E-mail: debi.lawson@bellsouth.com.

Robin List lives on a small farm in the Wairarapa province of New Zealand, and ministers at St. Andrew's church in the nearby village of Greytown. He has published two books of liturgical drama and another of Lenten studies, which explore lifestyle issues, using games to get into the subject matter (visit www.polygraphianz.com). He is currently writing a book connecting theology and intellectual disability. Robin is part of a set which includes Heather, their four children, one each of cat, dog, donkey, pet lamb, two each of horses and Dutch dwarf rabbits, as well as the animals who pay their way. Write to him at: West Bush Road, R.D. 8, Masterton, New Zealand. Phone: +64 6 370 8281. E-mail: donkey@wise.net.nz.

Shirley Lochowitz is the founder of "The Other End of the Barrel," an organization that addresses the issue of safe gun storage. She and her son continue to share their story in the hopes that these types of shootings will cease to exist. They recently completed a "The Other End of the Barrel" video. She is available for speaking engagements, and she can be reached by calling 262-989-4288 or by writing to P.O. Box 98, Franksville, Wisconsin 53126. Her website is: www.otherendofthebarrel.org.

Kenneth Lyerly retired from 23 years of active duty in the US Navy and has nineteen years of experience as a Drug and Alcohol Counselor. He has degrees in Psychology and Counseling. Ken is currently a local pastor serving United Methodist churches in Genoa City and Pleasant Prairie, Wisconsin. He and his wife, Betty, have been married for 41 years and have three grown children, two girls and a boy. Write to him at: 7937 30th Avenue, Kenosha, Wisconsin 53142. Phone: 262-694-1468. E-mail: klyerly@wi.rr.com.

Patricia Lyon is lead pastor for the Whitewater Area Regional Ministry in Whitewater, Wisconsin. Her congregation serves over 320 university students a free lunch on Tuesdays, and they host a developing Hispanic ministry. The church has received an award for excellence from the Lily Foundation. Pat is a grandmother and a gardener who lives with three Persian cats. For the past three summers, Pat has traveled to Cambodia as a volunteer to make peace and teach English. She and the other missioners fund the project with rummage sales, concerts, and soliciting donations from friends and relatives. E-mail: plyon@wisconsinumc.org.

Penny McCanles is a member of Wauwatosa Avenue United Methodist Church in Wauwatosa, Wisconsin. She operates a home-based business as a communications consultant, but her real love is creative writing, especially poetry. She can be reached by e-mail at pmccanles@wi.rr.com.

Kai McClinton is a native of Milwaukee, Wisconsin, whose spiritual journey began the day of her baptism. She spent years working for and following Christ in her home church, St. James United Methodist Church. Kai heeded the call to ministry in 1996, graduated from Garrett-Evangelical Theological Seminary in 1999, and has served as pastor of Solomon Community Temple United Methodist Church in Milwaukee for the past four years. E-mail: kaim@prodigy.net.

Lee Meissner is pastor of Christ United Methodist Church of Watertown, Wisconsin, and has served United Methodist Churches

in central and southwest Wisconsin since 1976. He received his Master of Divinity and MAR degrees from the University of Dubuque Theological Seminary in Dubuque, Iowa. Write to Lee at 518 Carl Schurz Drive, Watertown, Wisconsin 53098.
E-mail: helenm@ticon.net.

Doris Miller is a native Mainer, and a graduate of The Wharton School of the University of Pennsylvania. She attended the Course of Study School of Wesley Theological Seminary. She has served as a local pastor for several years in the Troy Annual Conference in New York. Currently she serves as Coordinator of Educational Ministries at the Shenendehowa United Methodist Church in Clifton Park, New York. She is working toward deacon's orders. Her e-mail address is damfree@localnet.com.

Ralph Milton, broadcaster, publisher, engaging speaker, best-selling author and angel, has lived everywhere from rural Grass River, Manitoba, to urban New York, to exotic locales in the Philippines. His humorous, easy style makes him ever popular with audiences and readers alike. Co-founder of Wood Lake Books, Ralph now chooses to live in Kelowna, British Columbia, close to his grandkids and his peanut butter. He is the editor of "Rumors," a free newsletter for active Christians with a sense of humor, and moderator of Julian's Cell, an on-line discussion group about Julian of Norwich. To subscribe to "Rumors," send an e-mail to: rumors - subscribe@joinhands.com.

Jane Moschenrose, a graduate of Andover Newton Theological School, has served as pastor of Wellspring Church, an American Baptist Church, in Farmington Hills, Michigan, since 1998. She is married to Phillip and mother to Karen. You can reach her at 1133 Elliott Court, Madison Heights, Michigan 48071.
E-mail: jmoschenro@aol.com.

Robert Murdock, a retired farmer, lives with Mary, his wife of 52 years, on their farm in rural East Troy, Wisconsin. They have four children and six grandchildren, who are the family's seventh generation on the farm. Robert and Mary attend Little Prairie United

Methodist Church. Robert extends his gratitude to Pastor Lucinda Alwa for being a counselor and caring friend throughout his illness and recovery.

Linda Nafziger-Meiser is pastor of the Hyde Park Mennonite Fellowship in Boise, Idaho. She is the mother of two daughters, and is in the 25th year of marriage to her best friend. E-mail: lindanm@mindspring.com.

Roy Nelson is attending Wartburg Theological Seminary in Dubuque, Iowa, where he has relocated with his wife and two children. His home church is St. Matthews Evangelical Lutheran Church in Wauwatosa, Wisconsin. Roy is an attorney, mediator, arbitrator, and former police officer. E-mail: rhnmgn@wi.rr.com.

Nancy Nichols grew up in northern Indiana, the youngest of four daughters. She graduated from Valparaiso University and Garrett-Evangelical Theological Seminary, and was ordained in The United Methodist Church. Nancy received an M.A. in Adult Education at Ball State University in 1999, and is currently completing course work toward a doctorate in Adult, Higher and Community Education. She presented part of this story at the National Communications Association in New Orleans, Louisiana, in November, 2002. She is pastor of St. Paul's United Methodist Church in Muncie, Indiana, where she lives with her stately Old English sheepdog, Sir Winston Churchill, a beagle-basset named Scrub, and a basset hound, Clifford.

Debra Sumwalt Partridge grew up in Wisconsin and married a military man. She, her husband Kent, and their children Kent, Jr. and Wendi lived in North Dakota, Alabama, Okinawa, Japan, and Florida. In the Millbrook United Methodist Church, Millbrook, Alabama, she served in several officer positions in the United Methodist Women's group. Now living in Wisconsin, she currently loves her position as grandmother, traveling to California to spoil her grandchildren, Samantha, Rebecca, and Kristopher. E-mail: kpartridge@charter.net.

233

Timothy Paulson is the father of three children and is currently co-owner of Anchor Tile and Stone. He is an active member of Grand Avenue United Methodist Church in Port Washington, Wisconsin, where he has been part of missions and evangelism. He loves people and has a strong desire to share his faith through his story. E-mail: elmerfud3@hotmail.com.

Bill Penaz lives in Milwaukee, Wisconsin, and is a longtime member of Loving Shepherd Evangelical Lutheran Church.

Jo Perry-Sumwalt is Director of Christian Education at Wauwatosa Avenue United Methodist Church in Wauwatosa, Wisconsin. She has co-authored two books with John, *Life Stories,* '95 and *Lectionary Tales for the Pulpit,* '96. Besides John, writing, and their two grown children, Kati and Orrin, Jo's loves are needlework, furniture refinishing, antiquing, refurbishing their farm house, long walks with John, and their eight-year-old Westie, Eli. E-mail: jsumwalt@naspa.net.

Marie Regine Redig, S.S.N.D., a member of the School Sisters of Notre Dame, is a retreat and spiritual director. She is a member of Mary Queen of Martyrs Catholic Parish. Her story "A Sign of God's Love," appeared in *Vision Stories: True Accounts of Visions, Angels, and Healing Miracles.* Write to her at 4244 N. 50th Street, Milwaukee, Wisconsin 53216. E-mail: rredig@ssnd-milw.org.

Leslie Powell Sadasivan, a registered nurse from Strongsville, Ohio, was tragically brought into activism following the 1997 suicide of her gay son, Robbie Kirkland, during his freshman year in high school. Leslie, a devoted wife and mother to her four children, was moved to speak out about the pain and harassment her son endured from his peers. Leslie attends St. John Neumann Catholic Church in Strongsville. For more information about Robbie, see his website at www.lgcsc.org/robkirkland/index.html.

Jim Schlosser, a native of West Bend, Wisconsin, served three years in the military, then settled in his home town to serve his community in the field of public works. He is presently disabled with congestive heart failure, and spends most of his time reading and preparing for the Tuesday evening Bible group, the Christian Bible Fellowship, which he holds weekly in his home. Jim and his wife, Loxley, attend a local non-denominational church.

Elaine Scrivens was born in South Wales and attended Manchester University, where she obtained a Bachelor of Education degree. She and her husband, Jim, have three boys. Elaine trained for ministry on North East Ecumenical Course and was ordained by David, Archbishop of York, on Advent Sunday, 2000. At present she is Curate in the parish of Coatham and Dormanstown, a small parish in the North East of England, and also teaches full-time in a local High School. E-mail: elaine.scrivens@ntlworld.com.

Jackie Scully was born and raised in New Haven, Connecticut. Her leadership role in a statewide grassroots organization and candidacy for the Cheshire, Connecticut, town council earned her a place in The League Of Women Voters' *Women Who Have Made A Difference In The 90's*. Jackie, her husband Mike and their two children moved to Genesee, Wisconsin, in 2000. She spends her spare time volunteering in the community and pursuing her song writing. Her favorite song topics are God, family, love, and finding the humor in everyday living. "I have a feeling that God has a wonderful sense of humor!" She can be reached at: scullysongs@wauknet.com.

Christinia Seibel is pastor of St. Luke's Lutheran Church, ELCA, in Curtice, Ohio. She was ordained two years ago, a second career pastor, her first career having been as a wife and mother while working in the social services field. Phone: 419-836-6179. E-mail: boatlady@accesstoledo.com.

Ellen Sherry lives in Ellsworth, Wisconsin, where she and her husband have raised three children. She works as the Community Education Director for the Ellsworth School District.
E-mail: desherry@pressenter.com.

Kerri Sherwood has released eight albums including *as sure as the sun*, which has "angel you are" as one of its tracks. Kerri is a singer-songwriter, recording artist, and composer whose music is written about the stuff of real life. Her piano and vocal music is sold nationwide and is promoted across the country on radio, television, music contract services, and video. Kerri also spent over 21 years as a director of music at churches in New York, Florida, and Wisconsin, and taught choir for several years at the secondary level in public schools. Her music and her personal narrative on its inspirations and composition create an instant rapport with her audiences as she performs in theaters, festivals, and promotional appearances. Check out her website at www.kerrisherwood.com or call the recording label 800-651-SISU (7478) for more information on her albums and performance schedule.

David Michael Smith is a banker by day, author by night, and has published two books, *The Invitation* and *Stories from the Manger*. He is happily married to Geralynn and they reside in Delaware. For more information, visit his website: www.davidmichaelsmith.net.

Kay Boone Stewart is a novelist (*Trilogy, Chariots of Dawn,* E. Thomas Nelson, '92), poet (*Sunrise Over Galilee,* '93, *The Color Red,* '94), non-fiction writer (*Here's Help,* '93), collaborator (*Don Stewart Tips ...* '93, *Window Watchman 11,* CIN '97), artist (Kay Cards — 2001), music composer, harpist, vocalist, storyteller, member/deacon Presbyterian Church, *Who's Who/American Women* (2000), *Who's Who America* (2002). She can be reached at: P.O. Box 727, Brentwood, California 94513.

Judy Snyder Stout is pastor of Hopewell United Methodist Church in Frankfort, Indiana. She is the mother of six and has five grandsons and one granddaughter.

Bruce Stunkard is a circuit-riding United Methodist preacher serving Ellsworth, Hartland, and Diamond Bluff United Methodist Churches in northwestern Wisconsin. The father of two, Bruce is a teacher of the Enneagram, and enjoys woodworking, kayaking, searching for stones, and Lake Superior. Write to him at 520 River Hills Drive, River Falls, Wisconsin 54022. Phone: 715-425-1196. E-mail: brucestunkard@mediaone.net.

John Sumwalt is pastor of Wauwatosa Avenue United Methodist Church. He is the author of the best-selling CSS series, *Lectionary Stories,* '90, '91, and '92. John has co-authored two books with his wife, Jo, *Life Stories,* '95 and *Lectionary Tales for the Pulpit,* '96. He does storytelling, inspirational speaking, and retreats. Write to John at: 2044 Forest Street, Wauwatosa, Wisconsin 53213. Phone: 414-257-1228. Fax: 414-453-0702. E-mail: jsumwalt@naspa.net.

Steve Taylor is Director of Missions Development for the North Carolina Conference of the United Methodist Church. He is a Commissioned Missionary of the United Methodist Church who has served as a Church and Community Worker. Steve has worked in refugee relief in Slovenia and Croatia. He has served with Habitat for Humanity International, leading work teams in Vaz, Adony, and Budapest, Hungary. A twenty-year United States Air Force veteran, Steve is now an advocate for peace making and non-violence. He is married to Sheryl Bilski Taylor, and they have two children, Joy, 24 and Brett, 19, a grandson, Taylor, and son-in-law Sean Yancey. Steve is a frequent contributor to Desperate Preachers Site, a web-based community of preachers and teachers.

Pamela J. Tinnin is the pastor of Partridge Community Church — UCC, the only church in Partridge, Kansas (population 250). She was an editor at the University of California-Berkley, for ten years, a freelance writer, and a sheep rancher. Recently Pam collaborated with two United Methodist pastors on a collection of dramatic monologue sermons. The book will be released in the fall of 2004 by CSS Publishing Company.

Rosmarie Trapp is a member of the "Community of the Crucified One," 104 E. 11th Avenue, Homestead, Pennsylvania 15120. Rosmarie lives in an apartment in one of their mission houses in Vermont, where she is involved in children's Bible classes, fund raisers, and prison ministry, sharing the message, "Jesus loves you." Her family's story was told in the well-known movie, *The Sound of Music*.

Linda J. Vogel is Professor of Christian Education at Garrett-Evangelical Theological Seminary in Evanston, Illinois. She is a deacon in the United Methodist Church and is active at First United Methodist Church at the Chicago Temple. Her most recent books, co-authored with her spouse, Dwight, are *Sacramental Living: Falling Stars and Coloring Outside the Lines* (1999) and *Syncopated Grace: Times and Seasons with God* (2002), published by Upper Room Books. Write to her at: Garrett-Evangelical Theological Seminary, 2121 Sheridan Road, Evanston, Illinois 60201. E-mail: Linda.Vogel@garrett.edu.

Edeltraud Von Bruck was born and raised in a Christian home in Austria and continued her education, with degrees in French and Spanish, in the United States. She has served for many years as lay-counselor within the church and workplace. She has been employed as a teacher in various Christian schools, as counselor in children's institutions, and as governess and tutor, but her greatest love has been to share Christ and compose sacred songs. Although presently in New England, her previous home church was New Life Church in Colorado Springs, Colorado. She is the author of *Voyage: The Journey to Eternal Glory* (Creation House Press) and can be reached at P.O. Box 4222, Middletown, Rhode Island 02842.

Harold R. Weaver served William Street and Findlay Methodist Churches in the Ohio Conference before transferring to the Wisconsin Conference in 1964. Dr. Weaver served Wauwatosa Avenue United Methodist Church, First United Methodist Church in Madison, and Fifth Avenue United Methodist Church in West Bend before retiring in 1984. He helped to found the Milwaukee Theological Institute, an interracial and interdenominational school for religious studies. Dr. Weaver died in May of 2002.

Richard Whitaker, Diaconal Minister of Education at Whitefish Bay UMC in Milwaukee, Wisconsin, wishes to acknowledge all of those "seed planters" at his childhood home church, Epworth UMC, Savannah, Georgia, and all those spiritual companions at the Avondale-Pattillo UMC in Decatur, Georgia. Avondale's former pastor, Dr. Charles Hoover, is the one responsible for enabling Richard to hear God's call to the ministry of Christian Education.

Larry Winebrenner is Professor Emeritus of Miami-Dade Community College, after 33 years of teaching. He served as pastor of churches in Georgia, Florida, Indiana, and Wisconsin, retiring after thirteen years as pastor of York Memorial UMC in Miami. He still serves as Chaplain of Epworth Village Retirement Community in Hialeah, Florida. Larry has authored two college textbooks, served as an editor for three newspapers and an academic journal, and contributed articles to several magazines.

Andrea Woodard is a junior at the University of Wisconsin-Whitewater, majoring in early childhood education. She is the oldest of five children in the family of Jay and Laurie Woodard, which also includes Amanda, 18 and triplets Cassy, Becky, and John, 16. Her family attends First United Methodist Church in Waukesha, Wisconsin. Andrea has been involved in gymnastics for about fifteen years, and competes for her school, but her favorite activity is dancing.

Jenee Woodard is the author of the lectionary resource website "The Text This Week" (www.textweek.com). She teaches classes for clergy and lay people online and "live" around her home in Jackson, Michigan. She and her spouse, Bob, have two children, 14-year-old Jaie and 10-year-old Phil. She is also active in church, school, and community activities, and coaches gymnastics at the club her daughter attends. You can contact her at 3409 Loretta Drive, Jackson, Michigan 49201. Phone: 517-789-6676.
E-mail: jeneewd@textweek.com.

Amy Yarnall is pastor of Summit United Methodist Church in Middletown, Delaware. She has been in the local church since 1997. Amy is married and was blessed with her first child in April, 2002. Write to her at: 4725 Weatherhill Drive, Wilmington, Delaware 19808. Phone: 302-234-6999. E-mail: ashipster@aol.com.

Praise for *Vision Stories*,
John Sumwalt's previous collection of
true personal accounts of mystical experiences:

This wonderful collection of stories reminds us of a fact our world desperately needs to know — that God is alive and well and ready to be at work in our daily lives.
J. Ellsworth Kalas
Author of *New Testament Stories from the Back Side*

John Sumwalt has given us a treasury of God's meetings with the daily lives of people. Too often we think of God as hidden away in the stories of the Bible. Here we see God now encountering people in surprising ways of grace. May these stories encourage us to tell one another our stories of God's meetings with us as well.
Dwight Judy
Author of *Quest for the Mystical Christ*

I am very impressed with **Vision Stories** *as a resource for preaching, teaching, and spiritual formation reading. People, myself included, are hesitant to share holy moments which we think may seem strange to others. We fear they may not be received with the sanctity and gratitude which will always surround these moments for us. But others need to hear such stories, shared for no other reason than to witness to the reality of God in personal experience. This is what* **Vision Stories** *invites all of us to do. These stories help us to meet what may be the greatest spiritual need of our time — to know and to share the experience of the reality of God and the spiritual realm in a materialistic world.*
Charles R. Gipson
Author of *The Three-Year Community for Spiritual Formation*

Through stories and scriptural comparisons, Sumwalt offers insight into the extraordinary spiritual experiences of ordinary people.
Cheryl Kirking
Author of *Ripples of Joy*

Reading through these accounts forces the realization that the world in which we live is far more mysterious than we realize, and the realm of God's grace far deeper and richer than we can imagine. These experiences will be a great encouragement to many, especially those who have had such experiences but have thought they were abnormal.
M. Robert Mulholland
Author of *Shaped by the Word*

Vision Stories provides a breath of fresh air in a culture that often tries to smother even a hint of the mystical. These simple stories tell the profound truth that God is present and involved in the minute and major events of every life.
Bishop Reuben P. Job
Author of *A Guide to Spiritual Discernment*
Former editor, *The Upper Room*

*I am rejoicing as I read the testimonies in **Sharing Visions** and **Vision Stories**. What an inspiration! I recall my father, an unemotional man, telling me that his mother who had died some years before appeared to him in a dream and gave him counsel on a difficult decision he was wrestling with.*
Bishop Richard B. Wilke
Author of the *Disciple* Bible Study series